The Art of Love

The Art of Love

Ovid

Translated, with an Introduction, by
STANLEY APPELBAUM

Illustrated by
JEAN DE BOSSCHÈRE

DOVER PUBLICATIONS, INC.
MINEOLA, NEW YORK

Copyright

Bibliographical Note

This Dover edition, first published in 2010, contains a new complete translation
of Ovid's *Ars amatoria*, which first appeared ca. 1 B.C. and was first published in type
in 1471 (two separate editions, Bologna and Rome; see Introduction for details)
together with other works by Ovid. The illustrations, by Jean de Bosschère, are
taken from the volume *The Love Books of Ovid* . . . (translated by J. Lewis May),
published in 1930 by the Rarity Press, New York ("privately printed"); those on
pages ii, 3, 41, and 67 originally appeared in color. The present translation was made
by Stanley Appelbaum, who also wrote the Introduction.

Library of Congress Cataloging-in-Publication Data

Ovid, 43 B.C.–17 or 18 A.D.
    [Ars amatoria. English]
    The art of love / Ovid ; translated, with an introduction by Stanley Appelbaum ;
illustrated by Jean de Bosschère.
        p. cm.
    A new complete translation of Ovid's Ars amatoria.
    ISBN-13: 978-0-486-47660-5
    ISBN-10: 0-486-47660-X
    1. Didactic poetry, Latin—Translations into English. 2. Erotic poetry,
Latin—Translations into English. 3. Seduction—Poetry. I. Appelbaum,
Stanley. II. Bosschère, Jean de, 1878–1953. III. Title.
    PA6522.A8A75 2010
    871'.01—dc22

                                                                        2010018890

Manufactured in the United States by Courier Corporation
47660X01
www.doverpublications.com

CONTENTS

Introduction vii

Book One 1

Book Two 29

Book Three 59

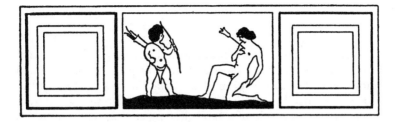

INTRODUCTION

I: Ovid's Life and Works

Background and Early Years. Ovid (Publius Ovidius Naso) was born into a moderately wealthy family of the equestrian order, and always lived on his family's money.

The *equites,* sometimes referred to as "knights," were a Roman social class much higher than the commoners (*plebs*) and only a little lower than the lofty *senatores;* an *eques* had to have a substantial minimum income. Originally the "equestrians" were Rome's cavalrymen; later they became a sort of minor nobility with special political prerogatives. Ovid had inherited his rank, but in his day—an era of quasi-Colonialist exploitation of conquered lands, in the aftermath of long, ruinous civil wars—the order was wide open to social-climbing businessmen and ambitious soldiers.

Ovid was born in 43 B.C. in Sulmo (today, Sulmona) in the Abruzzi hills some ninety miles nearly due east of Rome. Sent to the capital for his education, he put down solid roots there and became an urban playboy with heart and soul. After traveling through Greece, Asia Minor, and Sicily for his "finishing" (the equivalent of an eighteenth-century young British lord's Grand Tour on the Continent), he filled some very minor posts in the judiciary, but abandoned his political career before undertaking even the first of the major steps necessary for government advancement. He knew that he was a poet and that he wanted to devote his days to poetry, and he didn't need to kowtow to any public or private patron.[1]

---

[1]Much of what we "know" about Ovid's early years is based entirely on autobiographical statements that he himself published, largely in works dating from his banishment. In some parts of these works he was clearly exaggerating, doing special pleading, and even deliberately lying. The few data given above, however, seem trustworthy, although scholars shouldn't take all Ovid's declarations as gospel, as so many seem to do. [All the footnotes in this Introduction are exclusively devoted to speculations and polemics.]

Octavian, adopted son of Julius Caesar, had emerged from the civil wars on top of the heap, especially after his partisans had defeated Antony and Cleopatra at sea in 31 B.C., and the wealth of Egypt had landed in Roman laps. With the new name of Augustus (sacred, reverend) and the new title of *princeps* (leading citizen; rendered in this new translation as Prince, to reflect both the English word's etymology and Augustus's true status), he simulated modesty but was really an absolute dictator: the first Roman emperor. Some of the most promising Roman writers of the generation or two before Ovid had been pressed into national service and had written works flattering to Augustus and his lineage (particularly Vergil, with his *Aeneid*); but Ovid hadn't been an adult in the years of Augustus's ascension and subsequent "peacemaking," and he remained unbought and flippantly independent.

Works of the "First Period." From about 20 B.C., when his poems began to be published, until about 1 B.C., Ovid wrote witty love poetry: either verse in (mock?) adoration of specific women (perhaps imaginary), as in the *Amores* (Loves), or verse concerned with love and sex in one way or another, as in the *Heroides* (fanciful epistles written by famous "heroines" of myth and legend to their equally famous husbands or lovers). He also wrote a brief "instructional" work on ladies' cosmetics.

The pinnacle of this earliest output is the three books (scrolls) of the *Ars amatoria* (The Art of Love), newly translated in its entirety, in verse that simulates the original, in the present volume. This long poem will be the subject of section II of this Introduction.

Shortly after *The Art of Love* was completed, Ovid supplied one book of *Remedia amoris* (Cures for Love), in which he humorously offers men methods for breaking off relationships that are or have become tiresome or cumbersome. The advice includes: traveling (to "get away"), convincing yourself that your mistress is full of faults, initiating a new affair, etc. (A work from this period which was apparently noteworthy but is completely lost, was a play, *Medea*.)

"Second-Period" Writings. The first few years of what we call the A.D. era were devoted to two major works. Ovid's masterpiece and most influential creation, the *Metamorphoses*, in fifteen books, was composed entirely in hexameters (see section III of the Introduction for an explanation), his only major (and indisputably authentic) opus in that form. Always a storehouse of mythological lore, in the lengthy *Metamorphoses* Ovid concentrated entirely on myths involving transformations of people (into plants, animals, monsters, freaks, constellations, etc.).

Only the first half of the second major work of this period has come down to us. This was the *Fasti* (literally, "days of good omen on which public business may be conducted"), a collection of legends purporting to explain the origins of key dates in the Roman calendar, with one book (scroll) devoted to each month, beginning with January. The material for July through December was never published because of Ovid's apparently sudden banishment.[2]

Banishment and the "Third Period." In A.D. 8, Ovid was banished by a decree of Augustus, without a trial. This banishment was formally not an "exile," but a "relegation," a less dishonoring procedure in which the culprit retained his property and his civic rights (Ovid's wife, his third, loyally managed his financial affairs back in Rome). Relegation, however, did entail a specific place of permanent residence, and Augustus chose the city of Tomis, an old Greek colony on the Black Sea.

The ostensible reason for the relegation, it seems, was Augustus's displeasure with the morally corrupting influence of *The Art of Love*, but no one then or now has believed this; the work (and probably pieces by others that were more willfully pornographic) had been in circulation for almost a decade. Scholars usually accept Ovid's statements that he had committed some sort of blunder, not a crime: that he had seen something and not said something (that is, he had refused to turn state's evidence and inform on acquaintances who were under a cloud). With notable exceptions, scholars believe that Ovid was somehow implicated in the adulteries of Augustus's granddaughter Julia, for which she was exiled in the same year. (Like so many tyrants and reactionaries who harp on "family values," Augustus was himself

---

[2]Many scholars repeat the supposition that, in his banishment, Ovid was unable to do the necessary research for the second half of the *Fasti*. But there are strong indicators that he had already completed at least a first draft of it, and he did later undertake a halfhearted, cursory revision of the first half, changing the dedicatee from Augustus (presumably after the Prince's death in A.D. 14) to Germanicus, nephew of Augustus's successor Tiberius (from Germanicus he could still hope for a compassionate restoration to the fleshpots of Rome). In view of the scholarly consensus that the astronomy in the *Fasti* (a substantial component of the work) is frequently inaccurate and misunderstood, and in my own view that the work is desperately padded with narratives that are too frequent, far too long, and considerably dull and dry, I submit my rash opinion that the *Fasti* was an uncongenial jingoistic assignment imposed from above, and that the banished poet dropped it with a great sigh of relief!

a philanderer, though a very discreet one, and headed a particularly dysfunctional family.)[3]

The poet's enforced place of residence, Tomis (the form Tomi is now discredited), was one of the Black Sea colonies founded in the sixth century B.C. by people from the Greek city of Miletus (in the far west of Asia Minor) under pressure from the Persian empire of the Achaemenid dynasty. Its region had become the Roman province of Moesia ca. 30 B.C., when Augustus was attempting to establish the lower Danube as a bulwark against "barbarian" hordes. Situated some sixty-five miles southwest of that river's mouth, in the area now known as the Dobruja, Tomis stood where the present Romanian city of Constanţa now stands. The native population of the region, thinly overlain by Greeks and Romans, were chiefly Getae, with many Sarmatians and Thracians.

Ovid, a spoiled big-city worldling, generally professed to hate everything about Tomis, especially the cold, damp climate and some of his new neighbors (including wilder tribesmen who occasionally attacked the city walls and let off arrows). The two works he wrote at Tomis (partially on the way there) were the *Tristia* (Sorrows) and the *Epistulae ex Ponto* (Letters from the Black Sea). These poems, though they contain occasional topographical, ethnographical, and autobiographical nuggets, are made unpleasant by the poet's unconvincing recantations and his unrelieved whining and cringing, in his vain efforts to be recalled to Rome. He died in Tomis in A.D. 17 or 18 (authorities differ).

---

[3]Traditionally, Ovid's relegation is viewed as a "bolt from the blue," but this might not be true. As early as *Cures for Love*, Ovid reported criticism of the morality of his love books, but professed not to be worried as long as the "occasional crab" wasn't the most powerful person in Rome [my translation]:

Recently, certain people have disapproved of my writings;
  judging by what they say, wanton and bold is my Muse.
Yet, so long as I pleasure folk, and am everywhere cited,
  let an occasional crab carp at my work as he likes!

There was certainly some pressure on Ovid already; but there is also reason to believe that Augustus's resentment, whatever its cause, was coming to a slow boil over the years until a pretext for action could be found. Perhaps Ovid balked at composing the *Fasti* (see footnote 2, p. ix). And at the very end of the *Metamorphoses*, Ovid boastfully predicts that that work would outlast even "Jove's anger." Taken literally, what would the phrase mean? A severe thunderstorm? If "Jove" is taken as a (not all that subtle) code for "Augustus," the passage makes more sense, and indicates friction prior to the banishment.

A few, comparatively negligible, short works or fragments (some of disputed authorship) are assigned to Ovid's years of relegation.[4]

II: Comments on *The Art of Love*

Basics. Books One and Two, addressed to men, were published about 1 B.C.; Book Three, addressed to women, perhaps a bit later. The first printed editions (of Ovid's complete works; each edition in two folio volumes) both appeared in 1471: in Bologna (published by Balthazar Azoguidi) and in Rome (published by Sweynheym and Pannarz). The first English translation appeared in 1612, though (just possibly) there was no complete English version before the early twentieth century.

The Art of Love has been called "perhaps Ovid's most accomplished early work, with an assured mastery of the verse medium and an unflagging inventiveness and zest." It "gathers up and systematizes the erotic precepts which had gradually been developed (largely under Greek influence) by the Roman poets." Ovid is here concerned with love, not as a genuine passion, but as a social game. Sex partners are to be "picked up" in public or scouted at private gatherings; the book is about "making out" and "scoring" in cynically casual affairs based on physical attraction. (Men are not expected to support their mistresses; in fact, Ovid seems to have had a real phobia against giving even small gifts!) But there's relatively little (unlike the *Kāmasūtra*, for instance) in the way of sex positions or soft porn. There are playful quotations and parodies of passages in Homer and Vergil.

Book One of *The Art of Love* teaches men how to locate and win sex partners. Book Two teaches men how to hold onto the women they have won (for as long as it suits them). Book Three offers women advice equivalent to that offered to men in the first two books. (Incidentally, one poem in the *Loves* already contained a bawd's instructions to women.)

---

[4]Though Tomis naturally had far less to offer than Rome in the way of "culture" and "refinement," here again scholars are too quick to trust all the views expressed by the poet. After all, Tomis *was* a Greco-Roman site of long standing, and the metropolis of a significant grain-producing region; even Ovid admits he was well received and well treated there (at least until some of his hosts may have been soured by his endless outpouring of censure). And he learned to respect the Getae to the extent of writing a (now lost) poem in their language! His banishment was therefore not the unrelieved misery he often declares it to have been.

Writing from Tomis, Ovid insisted (deliberately misquoting himself) that the women he had had in mind in *The Art of Love* were only courtesans, ex-slaves, or loose-living plebeians, and never legally married Roman matrons. Actually, he alludes to or addresses various classes of women in various passages, but husbands are frequently mentioned (as fools to be duped), and only women of high social standing could afford much of the jewelry, cosmetics, and clothing he recommends as allurements.

Mythology. Narrative sequences were always part of Ovid's literary arsenal, and *The Art of Love* contains several notable, and sometimes beautiful, examples of myths and legends recounted at some length—but never excessively. Whether Ovid tells a fuller story or merely alludes to a myth glancingly, he uses mythology to back up his assertions in the way that a Christian preacher lards his homilies with citations from the Bible. (For the way that mythology is handled in this translation, see section III.)

The Topography of Rome: Porticos. "Rome now is golden," Ovid remarks sarcastically, seeming to echo Augustus's propaganda about his extensive building campaigns.

Four porticos (colonnades, covered passages, arcades, "porches") are mentioned in *The Art of Love*. Pompey's Portico was very near that great general's theater (see "Theaters," below). The Portico of Octavia, Augustus's sister, in memory of her son Marcellus (died 23 B.C.), was just north of the Theater of Marcellus (see below). The Portico of Livia, Augustus's second wife, built in her honor in 7 B.C., was somewhat to the northeast of the place where the Colosseum was later built, and very little to the northeast of the (even later) Baths of Trajan. The Portico of the Danaids, portraying the forty-nine women of Lemnos who murdered their husbands, was part of the splendid temple of Apollo that Augustus had built near his own house on the Palatine hill.

Theaters. There were three main theaters in operation in Ovid's day. Pompey's Theater, the first permanent stone-built one in Rome, was finished in 55 B.C. and was a model for subsequent ones. The Theatrum Balbi was built by Lucius Cornelius Balbus, a friend of Augustus, and dedicated in 13 B.C. The Theater of Marcellus, on the east bank of the Tiber just opposite the island in the river (today's Isola Tiberina), was built by Augustus in memory of his nephew and son-in-law; it was completed by 11 B.C., and there are extensive remains. Balbus's theater was somewhat to the northwest of Marcellus's, and Pompey's to the northwest of Balbus's.

All three theaters were located in the rather extensive plain between the left (east) bank of the Tiber and the western sides of the Pincian, Quirinal, and Capitoline hills. This area, which had been much built over in the course of the centuries, was contained in the upper semicircle of the huge **S** formed by the Tiber as it flows through the heart of Rome: an area known as the Campus Martius (Field of Mars). Even in Ovid's day there was still enough open space left for physical exercise there, including horseback riding.

Racecourses. When Ovid was writing—though there was also the very old Circus Flaminius in the Field of Mars, north of Octavia's Portico, then used mainly for miscellaneous shows—the "Circus" referred to is the Circus Maximus (often altered over the centuries; given the form known to Ovid by Julius Caesar), the chariot-racing venue in the valley between the Palatine and Aventine hills. Drivers would come as close as they dared to the turning-posts at either end of the tall median barrier. A poem in the *Loves* had already taught men how to break the ice with women at the Circus.

The Forum Romanum. This Forum (marketplace) par excellence (there were already separate markets elsewhere for cattle and produce) was a hallowed seat of government, containing lawcourts and the Senate house (Curia); the Via Sacra (Sacred Way) ran through it. Before the Colosseum was opened to the public in A.D. 80, gladiatorial fights were sometimes held in the Forum Romanum on sand that had been strewn there.

Temples. The temple of Venus Genetrix (Ancestress, Matriarch; the patron goddess of the Julian clan) was in Augustus's Forum Iulium, just north of the Forum Romanum; adjacent to it was the fountain that received its waters from the aqueduct known as the Aqua Appia (and thus the "abode of Appian nymphs").

The temple of Isis that was built in the reign of Caligula (A.D. 37–41) was in the Field of Mars, a little to the east of the Pantheon; in Ovid's day Isis's shrine was evidently surrounded by exercise grounds in the same general area. The cult of Isis was already very popular with Roman women. During the last centuries B.C., even in Egypt, the maternal role of Isis had been emphasized; there was something like mass production of metal figurines of the seated goddess tenderly holding her infant son Horus on her lap—precursors, both conceptual and visual, of later representations of the Virgin Mary with the Christ Child. (In Ovid's poems, Isis is often confused with the Greek maiden Io, seduced by Jupiter and transformed into a cow.)[5]

The temple of Hercules and the Muses was in the Circus Maximus area.

The temple of Vesta was located on the Via Sacra in the Forum Romanum. In Ovid's day, she also had a "chapel of ease" (for Augustus's ease) in the Prince's house on the Palatine (near the temple of Apollo already mentioned in the subsection on porticos, above).

The rites of the Good Goddess (Bona Dea; a fertility deity), from which men were excluded, were celebrated in the homes of high officials.

Miscellaneous. The mock sea battle sponsored by Augustus in imitation of the fifth-century B.C. battle of Salamis was staged in 2 B.C.

The Aqua Virgo (Waters of the Virgin), completed by Augustus's friend Agrippa in 19 B.C., was a major aqueduct (still in use) which ended in the city at what is now world famous as the coin-filled Fontana di Trevi.

The Parthians, an Iranian people who had taken over the Persian Empire from the Achaemenid dynasty, dwelling in what is now Iraq and Iran, were the official enemies of Rome in Ovid's day, the equivalents of Al Qa'ida and the Taliban at the time I write. Not only had the Parthians stubbornly resisted Roman encroachments; they had inflicted smarting defeats on the seemingly invincible Roman imperialists, especially when they captured Crassus's military eagle standards ("banners" in my translation) in 53 B.C. Augustus had won those back, but the Parthians remained contumacious; they were the enemies to be hated and cursed, and Gaius Caesar, a grandson of Augustus, was marching out against them. Ovid, for whom nothing was sacred, even makes a scurrilous comparison to the enemy's best-known tactic, the "Parthian shot": releasing deadly arrows at pursuers while retreating on horseback.

---

[5]Isis worship is referred to several times in *The Art of Love* and in at least half a dozen other places in Ovid's poems. Those authorities who state or suggest that there was no formal worship of Isis in Rome before Caligula's reign evidently believe that Ovid was delusional.

III: The Original Versification and the Present Translation

Elegiac Couplets. The couplet (pair of lines) known in classical Greek and Latin poetry as "elegiac" (the etymology is disputed; originally it may have been a loanword meaning "flute song") consists of one (dactylic) hexameter line followed by one (dactylic) pentameter line.

In English verse, meter depends on word or phrase stress; but in Greek and Latin, meter was based on the "quantity" of syllables: a given syllable was unalterably either long or short. A long syllable was long either "by nature" (intrinsically), when it contained an intrinsically long vowel or a diphthong, or else "by position," when its short vowel was followed by more than one consonant, whether those consonants were in its own word or in its own plus the consecutive word. In the first Latin word of *The Art of Love*, "Siquis," the first *i* is long by nature; the second one, short. In dactylic hexameters, the last of the six "feet" always consisted of two syllables, the first long and the second either long or short. The rest of the feet were all theoretically dactyls (– ˘ ˘), but all the dactyls, except for the fifth foot, could be replaced by spondees (– –). In pentameters, the "fifth foot" was split into one long syllable ending the first half of the line, and a final syllable that could be either long or short. The dactyl preceding the very last syllable had to be retained, whereas the first three dactyls could be replaced by spondees. The following metrical scheme resulted:

$$– \widetilde{\ \ } \,|\, – \widetilde{\ \ } \,|\, – \widetilde{\ \ } \,|\, – \widetilde{\ \ } \,|\, – \smile\smile \,|\, – \,\smile$$
$$– \widetilde{\ \ } \,|\, – \widetilde{\ \ } \,|\, – \,|\, – \widetilde{\ \ } \,|\, – \smile\smile \,|\, \smile$$

This left the poet considerable flexibility of rhythm. *H* didn't count as a consonant. (Fortunately, the additional rules and subtleties can be safely omitted from this rudimentary exposition.) Thus, the first two original lines of *The Art of Love*,

Siquis in hoc artem populo non novit amandi,
    hoc legat et lecto carmine doctus amet,

are "scanned" (graphed metrically) as follows:

$$\overline{\text{Si}}\breve{\text{quis}}\,\breve{\text{in}}\,|\,\overline{\text{hoc}}\,\overline{\text{ar}}\,|\,\overline{\text{tem}}\,\breve{\text{popu}}\,|\,\overline{\text{lo}}\,\overline{\text{non}}\,|\,\overline{\text{novit}}\,\breve{\text{a}}\,|\,\overline{\text{man}}\,\overline{\text{di}},$$

$$\overline{\text{hoc}}\,\breve{\text{legat}}\,|\,\overline{\text{et}}\,\overline{\text{lec}}\,|\,\overline{\text{to}}\,|\,\overline{\text{carmine}}\,|\,\overline{\text{doctus}}\,\breve{\text{a}}\,|\,\breve{\text{met}}.$$

Enjambement (continuation of syntactic clusters past the end of a line) can occur between the hexameter and the pentameter, but each couplet is syntactically end-stopped.

Elegiac Verse. In ancient poetry, the chosen meter usually reflected the topic. Elegiac verse, or elegy (associated only occasionally with mourning!), arose in Greece about 650 B.C., and nearly from the very outset was used for a variety of subject matter, including both expressions of love and instruction, or advice. In the Hellenistic, or Alexandrian, period (roughly 330–30 B.C.; especially influential on Roman poets), elegy was largely used for love poems and mythological narratives. According to Roman tradition, the form was introduced into Latin by the versatile poet Ennius (239–169 B.C.). In the early centuries A.D., it was used chiefly for epigrams.

In Ovid's day, elegiac couplets were unshakably associated with love poems, thanks to the work of his immediate predecessors Tibullus, Propertius, and Gallus (Gallus's oeuvre has been lost), and Ovid makes mock apologies when using the form for different purposes (as in the *Fasti*). At the very beginning of the *Loves*, he claims amusingly that he had set out to write in straight hexameters throughout (thus, to write a national epic like the *Aeneid*), but that cupid had stolen a (metrical) foot from every other line (thus converting the work into love poetry). By the time he wrote *Cures for Love*, he was able to boast that elegy was as indebted to him as epic was to Vergil.

This New Translation. The elegiac couplet, especially in the catchy, clipped rhythm of the pentameters, lends itself admirably to epigrammatic utterances or to a "sting in the tail." In Ovid's mischievous hands, the very meter adds to the fun. Therefore, I felt not merely tempted, but actually compelled, to offer a new English rendition that would (at least remotely) simulate the Latin prosody (metrical scheme), rather than using prose (always a betrayal of a poet, and useful only for overly literal students' aids), or shorter English lines ending in jingles (safe only for a Dryden or a Pope, if even then), or else insufficiently controlled "free verse." The present translation has precisely the same number of lines (and couplets) as the Latin original. Vast differences in syntax between Latin and English made it necessary very frequently to interchange material between hexameter and pentameter within a given couplet, but only once did I find it unavoidable to redistribute material over the length of two couplets.

In his references to myths, legends, history, geography, and Roman rites and customs, Ovid uses numerous alternative names, epithets, oblique allusions, and paraphrases (his alternative appellations are partly for the sake of the Latin meter, partly to introduce variety, but mainly to show off). In this new translation, the basic proper names of people and places are always used, and the allusions very briefly explained. For example, in line 17 of the poem, Ovid refers to Achilles as Aeacides ("descendant of Aeacus"; Aeacus was the hero's paternal grandfather); I give "Achilles." In the many instances where Ovid tosses off a cultural reference that he expects his "refined" readers or listeners to catch on the fly, I tacitly introduce some very concise elements of identification or expansion— but never adding to the number of lines or passing the limits of a couplet!

To recount each mythological story more fully would require a forest of forbidding footnotes, or the extension of this Introduction to double or triple its length. Intrepid readers desirous of further information are referred to such handy works as the often reprinted *Lemprière's Classical Dictionary*, which also indicates the original ancient sources of the myths.

Let me be the first to admit that my occasional recasting of the text in the ways indicated, giving its import and implications rather than a word-for-word replication (which would not be beyond the powers of even a relative beginner), sometimes makes the "translation" seem more like an "adaptation." But this was a conscious choice, and I unrepentantly prefer this approach to a pedantic rendering (which is used, and left completely only unannotated, in some translations).

The Illustrations. The illustrations in this volume have been taken over from the volume *The Love Books of Ovid*, "privately printed for" the Rarity Press, New York, 1930, which contains a creditable prose translation. The artist was Jean de Bosschère (ca. 1880–1953), Belgian-born, but long active in England (he also worked in France and Italy).

Between 1907 and 1923, the artist (also a watercolorist and engraver, in the Symbolist tradition of the late nineteenth century) illustrated over a dozen books that he wrote himself; the subject matter included ancient buildings and the folklore of Flanders. Later, in a style that has been called "neat and concise," a style that "eschewed unnecessary detail," he illustrated a number of translations into English that were published in London and New York. These include works by Ovid, Apuleius, Boccaccio, Rabelais, Baudelaire, Flaubert, and Wilde—all authors who, in the Prohibition era, were considered titillating, saucy, naughty, and risqué.

In his Ovid illustrations (some of which, at least, were apparently

published as early as 1925), de Bosschère was obviously strongly influ-
enced, at a distance, by Aubrey Beardsley's incomparable illustrations
for Wilde's *Salome*. The present Ovid drawings are more atmospheric
than strictly illustrative (for example, they contain considerably more
nudity than the text calls for); they are suggested, rather than dictated,
by the literary work.

The highly respected, and very busy, artist was also a personal
friend of some of the foremost writers of the time.

The Art of Love

BOOK ONE

All who are eager to know the surefire rules of romancing,
    make this manual yours! Learn how to conquer in love!
Vessels are rapidly moved by skill in sailing or rowing;
    skill makes chariots dash; love must be governed by skill.
How could Achilles go wrong with Automedon driving his war-car?
    Tiphys was born to steer *Argo*, that old Grecian ship:
Venus appointed yours truly to supervise Cupid's achievements.
    People will call me some day "helmsman and driver of Love."
Cupid is wild, to be sure, and often apt to be stubborn,
    but he's young, and youth's pliable, easy to rule.
Chiron the centaur once instructed Achilles in music,
    bending that warlike mind calmly with consummate art.
Foes and friends alike Achilles frightened when bigger,
    but we're told he cringed, fearing that elderly man.
Hands which Hector would feel, Achilles, when ordered by Chiron,
    held out meekly for blows after mistakes on the lyre.
Chiron taught that hero, and *I* am the teacher of Love,
    both being headstrong boys, both of them goddesses' sons.
Yet at last the ox submits his neck to the plowman,
    mettlesome horses clamp bridle-bits in their teeth;
Love will succumb to *me*, though he pierces my breast with his arrows,
    yes, even though he shakes torches of fire in the air!
Come, Love, shoot at me more: the more you recklessly hurt me,
    all the greater revenge *I* shall exact for my wounds!
No, Apollo, I'll never lyingly claim that *you* taught me,
    claim that I heard some bird prompting me while it flew by,

1

claim that, like Hesiod, I once saw Clio the Muse and her sisters
    while I shepherded flocks down in the valleys of home.
This book is based on knowledge: take the advice of an expert!
    All's true: mother of Love, kindly smile on my task!
Keep away, slender hairbands (prudish ladies' adornments);
    keep away, flounces that hide half of a "good" woman's feet!
Let me sing loves that are safe and "thefts" that are readily granted;
    here in my poem no gross wrongdoing secretly lurks.
First of all, let me tell you soldiers new to such weapons:
    seek out a lady to love, *that* is your primary task.
Secondly, you must strive to win her good grace with your wooing.
    Thirdly, make sure it's a love likely to last for a while.
These are the limits in which my chariot plans to maneuver,
    this is the post I'll graze lightly with swift-turning wheels.

While you still may, while yet you're able to roam about freely,
    choose which lady you'll tell: "*You* are the one meant for me."
Never expect her to drop right into your lap from the heavens;
    she who will please your eyes has to be looked for, and hard!
Hunters for deer know just where to spread the nets for their quarry,
    boar hunters know in which valley they're gnashing their tusks.
Hunters for birds know their thickets, and men who handle the fishhook
    know which waters they'll find brimming with succulent prey.
Likewise, you who are hunting for love and enduring affection,
    start off by learning just where ladies are wont to be found.
Searches like this don't involve your setting sail in the breezes,
    nor will your search demand roving down infinite roads.
Perseus may have carried off Andromeda out of the dark East;
    Paris, that lad of Troy, may have snatched Helen from Greece:
right here in Rome *you'll* find such a wealth of beautiful women,
    you'll say: "All that the world possibly offers is here!"
Many the fields on Mount Ida, and many the vineyards on Lesbos,
    many the fish in the sea, many the birds in the bush,
many the stars in the heavens—and *that* many belles in the city!
    Venus is based in the town known for Aeneas, her son.
Should you prefer a virgin who's still quite young and in blossom,
    here she is, all complete, right in front of your eyes.

Should you prefer fully grown young ladies: thousands and thousands!
    Men find it hard to decide just which one they should choose.
Should your taste run to quite mature age brackets, and wisdom,
    take it from me: here, too, numbers of them will be found.

Just take a leisurely stroll in the shade of Pompey's cool Passage
    while the summer sun enters the lion's sign;
stroll where Augustus's sister has added gifts to her son's gifts:
    down Octavia's Porch, clad in a rich marble coat.
Never avoid that Passage, adorned with old-master paintings,
    named for its patroness, great Livia, wife to the Prince,
nor that Porch where the Danaid girls plan to slaughter their cousins
    while their grim sire stands drawing his bloodthirsty sword.
Go on the day of Adonis, still wept for in Venus's temple,
    go on the Sabbath day worshipped by Syrian Jews.
Go to the temple of linen-clad Isis, that heifer of Memphis:
    ravished by Jove, she persuades girls to behave just the same.
Though it's hard to believe, even courtrooms are suited to wooing;
    flames of passion leap up even where trials are held:
there where the nymph beneath the marble temple of Venus
    strikes the air with her jet spurted from Appian founts,
there in that very spot Love overtakes the attorney;
    he who once pled for the rest now cannot plead for himself.
There in that very spot words fail the eloquent speaker;
    on comes a brand-new case, one where the trial is *his*.
Venus, from her adjacent temple, now laughs at his troubles:
    advocate not long ago, *he* needs a counselor now.

Yet, round theaters are best locations for amorous hunting;
    places like these repay prayers and vows best of all.
There you will find some woman for loving, or one for deceiving;
    some you may toy with just once, some you may want to retain.
Just as a long line of ants go back and forth on their labors,
    clasping their usual food tight in their grain-bearing beaks,
just as the bees revisit their fragrant meadows and pastures,
    flying amid the blooms, over the top of the thyme,
thus do lady sophisticates flock to a show that's successful:

such are their numbers, my mind often has ground to a halt!
Though they come to look on, they also come to be looked at:
    that's a place which dooms chastity, modesty, shame.
Romulus, first Roman king, first troubled the civic arena:
    Sabine women were snatched, wives for the bachelors of Rome.
Back then, theaters weren't of marble or shaded by awnings,
    nor were the platforms then yellowed by light-flowing paint;
foliage from the trees on the wooded Palatine hillside
    lay there with no show of art; all unadorned was the stage;
people sat in the turf-built rows of that primitive theater;
    any old leaves they could find covered their shaggy long hair.
Each man looked all around, locating the wife of his wishes,
    thinking many a thought deep in his taciturn heart.
Then an Etruscan flutist gave out with a plain, simple rhythm;
    thrice the performer's foot stamped on the flattened-down earth;
everyone started to clap (applause in that era was artless);
    Romulus gave the sign: now was the moment to act.
Forth they leapt, their savage cries proclaiming their ardor,
    seizing with lustful hands maidens and matrons alike.
Just as a timid flock of pigeons will fly from an eagle,
    just as a baby lamb flees from the wolf that it fears,
thus those women dreaded the men rushing wildly to seize them;
    all the color drained fully from each woman's cheeks.
One fear all of them shared, but they showed it in very distinct ways:
    some of them tore their hair, some sat mindlessly still.
Some were wordless with sorrow, while others called vainly for Mother;
    some lamented, some fled, others mutely remained.
Some were led away as prey for the marital bedstead;
    many of them were lent grace by the fear they displayed.
Some women struggled too hard, rejecting unwanted companions:
    off they were borne by the men, off in their lustful embrace.
"Why," said the men, "do you spoil those tender eyes with your weeping?
    What to your mother your sire, *that* will *I* be to you."
Romulus, you alone knew what booty to offer your soldiers;
    give the same booty to me, watch me go soldiering, too.
Naturally, since that day our theaters have flashed the same message:
    nowadays, too, they prove places where women are caught.

★

Don't stay aloof from the races, those sprints of thoroughbred horses;
    tracks that hold plenty of folk offer particular boons.
There you've no need to keep your secrets by speaking with fingers,
    there you've no need to nod, showing you've noticed some sign.
Sit right next to your lady, for no one there will forbid it;
    snuggle up side to side just as close as you can.
Lines that mark off the seats will join you and her willy-nilly,
    thankfully, seatmates touch: such is the plan of the place.
Now is the time to think and search for an opening gambit:
    words that the public can hear ought to be uttered at first.
Zealously ask the miss if she knows whose horses are running;
    quickly, whomever she likes, tell her that *you* like him, too.
Then, at the long parade of ivory statues of godheads,
    first and foremost applaud Venus with favoring hands.
Should, as it often happens, a speck of dust fall on the lady's
    lap, flick it off at once, using your fingers to flick.
Should no dust appear, still flick it as if it *had* fallen.
    All that occurs should become cause for some action by you.
Should her mantle slip down and lie at her feet on the ground there,
    gather it up, lift it up eagerly out of the dirt.
Thanks to this service, at once she'll surely become more permissive,
    granting your eyes a quick glimpse of her sought-after legs.
Once again, look all around to see that no nuisance behind you
    presses her tender back roughly with ruffian's knees.
Little things please little minds, and many have found it quite useful
    deftly to rearrange cushions, thus giving her ease.
Likewise of great advantage is fanning her lightly, and also
    slipping beneath her feet gently a comforting stool.

Such approaches the racecourse provides for budding romances;
    nevertheless, don't neglect shows on the Forum's sad sands:
there, as a gladiator, the son of Venus does battle;
    spectators watching the wounds shout out that *they're* wounded, too.
Speaking to *her* and touching her hand and requesting the program,
    placing a bet as you ask, "Which man is likely to win?,"
wounded yourself, you groan as you feel the force of Love's arrow,
    finding that you yourself now are a part of the show.

★

Recently, Prince Augustus arranged for a mock naval battle,
      bringing in Persian ships, vessels of Athens as well.
Young men from both our coasts arrived here, and so did young women,
      all the populous world filling Rome to the brim.
Who was unable to find a lady to love in that crowd then?
      Love from a stranger pained many a heart at the time!

See now, Augustus is planning to finally fill up a blank space
      left in the empire's map; Orient, you shall be ours!
Parthians, pay the price for slaying Crassus! Rejoice now,
      banners that once were clutched tight in barbarian hands!
Vengeance is nigh, a young leader proclaims that, his youth notwithstanding,
      war he is ready to wage, war that's too rugged for boys.
Timorous citizens, cease to total the sum of gods' birthdays:
      speaking of Caesars, expect courage to come in advance.
Men of godlike temper outrace their calendar ages,
      finding it hard to brook slothful effects of delay.
Small as he was, the Greek hero strangled two snakes in his cradle:
      Hercules showed even then valor befitting Jove's son.
Bacchus, who still are a boy, how big were you then when you conquered
      India, and instilled fear with your ivy-clad staffs?
Authorized by your father Agrippa, young lad, you'll do battle;
      guaranteed by *his* name, Gaius, you're certain to win.
Such a beginning you owe us, you bear a name of such import;
      now you are Prince of the Youth, some day the chief of the old.
Being a brother yourself, fight a king who ousted his brothers;
      being a hero's son, guard every one of his rights.
You've been armed by a man who's father of you and your country;
      Parthia's king has a throne snatched from his father (some son!)
You shall bear filial weapons, while *he* shall shoot criminal arrows;
      law and filial rights justly shall favor your cause.
Parthia loses its legal case; let it lose, too, in warfare.
      Add the wealth of the East, lad, to the coffers of Rome.
Father Mars and Father Caesar, shed grace on his going:
      one of you now is a god, one of you *will* be some day.
Victory I can foresee, a poem I vow and shall publish,
      praising all your deeds loudly in glorious song.

Gaius shall stand and exhort his soldiers in words of my making;
  let my words not fall short of the valor he shows!
Parthian backs retreating I'll sing, Roman breasts all advancing,
  arrows shot by a foe backward on galloping steed.
Parthians flee to conquer: what's left for them after they're conquered?
  Parthian gods of war even now prophesy doom.
Thus, that day shall come when, pleasuring every beholder,
  golden lad, you'll ride drawn by four snowy steeds.
Going before you, the vanquished come laden with chains on their shoulders,
  lest they flee as before, gaining their safety that way.
Happy, the young men of Rome will look on, with maidens among them;
  that great day will shed gladness on everyone's heart.
Then, when one of the women asks you the names of the monarchs,
  what the floats represent, places or rivers or hills,
answer her every query, and don't just wait for a question;
  even when you don't know, make up some answer at will.
That old man whose brow is bound with reeds: the Euphrates!
  that one with pendent blue locks: well, the Tigris is he!
Say that those over there are Armenians, others are Persians,
  say that that city there stood in Iranian vales.
This man or that man: a chief. And they'll all be just what you call them,
  accurately, if you can, otherwise suitably named.

Banquets are opportune, too; when you're lounging by well-laden tables,
  wine's not the only good thing to be sought and be found.
Frequently, luminous Cupid has wrestled with Bacchus, at parties,
  gently tugging his waist, gently squeezing his horns;
then, after wine has spattered Cupid's bibulous pinions,
  Cupid ceases and stands, weighed down by wine, on one spot.
Yes, to be sure, he rapidly shakes his liquid-logged feathers;
  nevertheless, it hurts hearts to be sprinkled by love.
Wine will perk up your courage and make you ready for passion;
  wine in quantity routs care and melts it away.
Then jolly laughter ensues; even paupers pluck up their valor;
  then all sorrows and woes flee, like wrinkles from brows.
Then sincerity, rarest of gifts in the age that we live in,
  opens our hearts, while the god chases off cunning and guile.

Frequently there the heart of some youth has been snatched by some lady;
  Venus, concealed in the wine, adds new fire to its fire.
Don't, at such times, be deceived by trusting too much in dim lamplight:
  wine and the darkness can warp judgments on women's good looks.
Paris, when judging the goddesses' beauty, was out in full daylight,
  saying to Venus: "You win; *you* are the fairest of all."
Nighttime cloaks their faults, allowance is made for each blemish;
  that time of day lends each lady the look of a queen.
Wait till daytime to judge the merits of gems or of dyed wool,
  wait until then to judge women's body and face.

Why count up all the places where ladies gather, those perfect
  hunting grounds? It's like counting the sands on the shore.
Why mention Baiae, that beach resort with its local regatta,
  famed as a spa where the smoke rises from sulfurous pits?
Someone, returning from there with a wounded heart, sadly told me:
  "Taking those waters was *not* good for me, praised as they are!"
Here we have, right in our suburbs, the temple of Woodland Diana,
  where each priest won his post killing the one there before:
she, a virgin who loathes the love-causing arrows of Cupid,
  gave men many a wound, surely will wound us again.

Thus far, carried along on the jolting wheels of two meters,
  Ovid has taught where to snare women, once they've been picked.
Now I plan to hone my art and teach you to trap them,
  so that the one you like winds up caught in your net.
Men! Whoever, wherever you are: pay strictest attention;
  commoners, favor me, heeding this, my deep lore.

First of all, you must have self-confidence: all of them *can* be
  captured, sure as a shot; just you spread out your nets!
Birds will sooner be mute in springtime, cicadas in summer,
  sooner will well-trained hounds turn their back on a hare,
than a well-wooed lady will offer resistance to lovers:
  even one you suppose out of your reach will give in.
Stolen love, so delightful to men, is more so to women;
  men reveal too much, women can hide their desire.

Should it behoove us males not to be the first to request love,
    women, already ours, gladly would step forth and ask.
Cows in grassy pastures attract the bulls with their mooing,
    mares are always seen whinnying low to the males.
Lust in humans is much less fierce, not half as much frantic;
    flames of passion in men keep to legitimate bounds.
Only reflect on Byblis, who burned with love for her brother
    (lawless love) and paid bravely for crime with a noose.
Myrrha adorned her father, but not like a dutiful daughter;
    now she's lost in the trees, myrrh bark closing her in.
(Those are her tears, you know, tears shed as arboreal fragrance,
    which perfume us, and still keep that heroine's name.)
Once, in the shady dells of forest-bearing Mount Ida
    lived a pure-white bull, glory of herds near and far;
save for one black spot between his horns (the sole blemish
    one could find on that bull), whiter than milk was the rest.
Heifers came from all over Crete, from Knossos and Cydon,
    hoping to have that bull mount them and give them some joy.
Queen Pasiphaë relished becoming a bovine adult'ress;
    envy gnawed at her heart, hatred for beautiful cows.
This is well known; though, Crete, you've a bad reputation for lying,
    land of a hundred towns, try to deny this event!
Queen Pasiphaë plucked fresh leaves and grass from the meadows,
    though her hands ere then never had turned to that task.
Joining the herd, she lost all shame, all thought of her husband;
    Minos, the king, then lost marital rights to the bull.
Queen, what need did you have to put on elaborate garments?
    That rough lover of yours cared not a jot for their cost.
What did a mirror avail when you sought out the herds on the mountains?
    Why, you fool, did you primp, brushing and combing your hair?
Why not believe your mirror, assuring you: "*You* are no heifer!"?
    How you'd have liked to have horns sprout from both sides of your head!
Being contented with Minos, why look all around for a lover?
    Wishing to cheat on a man, do so at least with a man!
Off she went into the woods, a queen deserting her bedside,
    just like a Maenad, wild, egged on by Bacchus the god.
Ah, how often she gave dirty looks to some cow, while exclaiming:

"Why does that lord of mine favor such commonplace beasts?
Just see them frisk in his sight on the tender grass in the pasture:
    there's no doubt but the fools think themselves full of appeal."
Saying this, she commanded one cow to be culled from the huge herd,
    ordering it to be yoked, though it had done nothing wrong.
One cow was brought to an altar and sacrificed there to no purpose;
    happily then the queen lifted its guts in her hands.
Many a time she appeased the gods by the death of her rivals;
    holding their entrails up, "Now go and please him!" she'd say.
Sometimes she wished to be Europa, at other times Io;
    one was a cow, one got carried away by a bull.
One day, that head of his herd, deceived by a cow made of maple,
    got the queen pregnant: a sire later betrayed by her young.
Cretan Aerope, had she abstained from sex with her husband's
    brother (and is it too much, doing without some one man?),
wouldn't have made the sun god, sickened by family sinning,
    change his course and drive backward into the dawn.
Scylla, who stole the purple hair from the head of her father,
    now has rabid dogs fixed to her womb and her groin.
King Agamemnon, escaping Mars on land, on the ocean
    Neptune, arrived back home, there he was slain by his wife!
Who has failed to lament Creusa of Corinth, Medea's
    victim; Medea herself, stained with the blood of her sons?
Phoenix, for love of a woman, was blinded one day by his father;
    chaste Hippolytus died torn by his terrified steeds.
Phineus, the king of Thrace, was tricked into blinding his children;
    then he suffered the same punishment, sent by the gods.
All those evils arose through the lustful emotions of women,
    sharper than men ever feel, fuller of madness and spite.
Therefore, take heart and expect them all to be pliant and yielding;
    many you'll try, out of all scarcely one will refuse.
Whether they say yes or no, they'll all be glad that you asked them:
    even though you fail, still there's no danger in that.
Yet, why should you fail when a new romance means new pleasure?
    Things not ours by right please us more than our own.
Other men's fields produce a crop that's better than *our* crop;
    isn't our neighbor's cow always richer in milk?

*

Let your first care be to meet with the coveted woman's
    servant girl, for *she* knows how to smooth your approach.
Make sure no one else is so close to her mistress's counsels,
    yet such a faithful ally, guarding your secretive sports.
Bribe her with promises, bribe her constantly, begging and praying;
    once she's willing, you'll gain easily all that you wish.
Just like a doctor who waits on occasions, *she'll* choose the right time,
    finding her mistress at ease, readily captured and won.
That will be when your woman, all her affairs in good order,
    blossoms out like a bush planted in fertile terrain.
Hearts that are filled with joy and not constricted by sorrow
    open up, and then Venus creeps artfully in.
Troy, when sad, defended itself with numerous weapons;
    joyful, it let in the horse laden with bloodthirsty men.
Also, make your attempt when she thinks that her husband is cheating;
    then, by your actions, make sure vengeance will come to her soon.
Let her maid urge her on, while combing her hair in the morning;
    let the vessel's sail speed with the aid of an oar.
Let the maid say "to herself," while sighing low in a murmur:
    "No, I imagine you won't pay back your husband in spades."
Then let her talk about *you*, let her put in words of persuasion,
    swearing she's watching you die, maddened by love as you are.
Hasten, don't let the sails fall slack or that wrath be abated:
    anger is lost by delay, melting away just like ice.
Is it a help, you ask, to seduce the servant herself? No,
    such a direful deed causes too much of a risk.
Bedding some maids makes them eager to help, while others grow sluggish;
    one maid will save you to please Mistress, and one for herself.
All is uncertain. Though sometimes fortune will favor bold ventures,
    take my advice and abstain, keeping your true goal in mind.
I'm not a climber of hills who traipses past headlong abysses;
    no young man led by me ever will end up as prey.
Yet, if the maid pleases you as she goes to and fro with your love notes,
    not by her service alone—no, by her body as well—
conquer her mistress first and then the servant girl after:
    never begin your affair taking the handmaid to bed.
This alone I insist on (provided you trust what I'm teaching,

no winds blowing my words recklessly outward to sea):
either you make no attempt or you persevere: maids won't betray you
    once they have shared in your guilt; then no informer remains.
Birds can't easily flee on wings that are coated with birdlime,
    boars can't lightly elude hunting-nets widely outspread.
Fish that are hurt by the hook after seizing it must be held onto:
    closely embrace your prize, don't back off till you've won.
Then she will never snitch; she finds herself equally guilty;
    then all her mistress's deeds, all of her words will be "spilled."
Keep the maid's secrets mum; if she's never revealed as your agent,
    gladly she'll serve as your spy, helping you get to your goal.

Should you suppose that the seasons are watched by dirt farmers only,
    should you suppose they concern sailors alone, you'd be wrong.
Grain's not entrusted at all times to fields (they can often deceive you),
    ships can't always sail waters of treacherous green.
Likewise, you're not always safe laying traps for delectable women;
    often, observing the date leads to a better result.
Should the day be *her* birthday, or the first-of-March celebration
    joining Venus to Mars (days when you need to give gifts),
should the Circus vendors display unusual trinkets,
    gifts of holiday class, presents suited for kings—
put it off! Wintry storms and the Pleiades threaten at such times;
    then the stars in the Kid drown in the watery deep.
Call a halt on such days, when anyone testing the ocean
    finds himself, after the wreck, clinging to flotsam alone.
Start on July eighteenth, when the sorrowful Allia river
    flowed with Roman blood shed by the conquering Gauls.
Start on the day when so many businesses put up their shutters:
    Sabbath day of the Jews, Palestine's favorite feast.
Hold as a day of particular dread your beloved one's birthday:
    days when you have to give gifts must be avoided with care.
Yet (do your best to avoid it!), she'll get something from you: a woman
    knows every way to extract coin from a love-smitten man.
Shabby hawkers will visit your loved one, who's fond of acquiring,
    there as you sit they'll display wares she can hardly resist.
You'll be asked to inspect them, a fancied expert in gewgaws;

after a tender kiss, *you'll* be expected to pay.
Swearing she'll be content for years and years with this purchase,
  swearing she needs it right now, Darling will tell you to buy.
Should you attempt to allege you don't have the money at home then,
  you'll be asked for a note (aren't you glad you can write?).
What if she claims it's her birthday and wants some cash for a pastry?
  What if her birthday returns each time it suits her to say?
What if she's plunged into grief for a loss that's merely a pretext,
  swearing a precious stone fell from the hole in her ear?
Women request many items as loans, but refuse to return them;
  lost to you, they bring no recompense for the loss.
Had I ten months, and tongues in equal number, I couldn't
  tell all the wanton wiles practiced by cash-hungry whores!

Let inscribed waxed tablets precede you when testing the waters,
  letters revealing your thoughts, suited for blazing your trail.
Let them transmit your praising, in close imitation of lovers;
  also, whoever you are, add entreaties galore.
Swayed by the old man's urging, Achilles gave Hector to Priam;
  even wrathful gods yield to an eloquent prayer.
Make a lot of promises, for what harm can promises cause you?
  Anyone's able to look rich by promising much.
Once Hope dwells in the human heart, it's always enduring;
  false though that goddess prove, nevertheless she takes hold.
After you've given a gift, you'll likelier find yourself jilted;
  now what you've given is hers; what has she lost by the deal?
Things, though, you haven't given—behave as if ready to give them:
  that way, a barren field often deceives farmer folk.
Gamblers who try not to lose can pile one loss on another;
  often they clutch their dice tightly in covetous hands.
"This is the hardship, the toil": to win her love without presents;
  fearing her previous grants useless, she'll grant even more.
Therefore, keep sending letters composed of flattering phrases,
  testing her state of mind, trying to feel out the path.
Borne on an apple, a message deceived Cydippe, who, reading
  oaths of love aloud, had to abide by her words.

★

Learn the art of rhetoric, youth of Rome, I adjure you,
    not so much to assist trembling defendants in court:
just like the commons or learned judges or lords of the Senate,
    women, won by words, sink in an orator's arms.
Only, conceal your powers, don't spout like an eloquent jurist:
    let your writings avoid words that she won't understand.
Who that isn't a fool would declaim to his tender beloved?
    Often a pompous note leads to a lifetime of hate.
Let your letters contain believable, everyday language,
    yet so persuasive, you'll seem right there, chatting away.
Should she refuse to accept your note and return it unopened,
    hope that she'll read it some day; keep to the purpose in mind.
Passage of time makes recalcitrant oxen yield to the plowman,
    time makes horses obey tugs on the flexible reins.
Iron rings wear out at last through sedulous usage;
    plowshares waste away, constantly turning up earth.
What can be harder than stone, or what can be softer than water?
    Yet, the hardest stone's hollowed by water that drips.
Even the chaste Penelope, steadily wooed, can be conquered;
    Pergamus, often besieged, needed time, but it fell.
What if she's read your letter, but won't write back? Never force her;
    just make sure that she keeps reading cajolements from you.
Women who've deigned to read a letter will finally answer;
    things of this type proceed slowly, by gentle degrees.
Maybe her first reply will discourage you, maybe annoy you,
    saying she hopes you won't pester her constantly so.
Yet, what she asks, she fears; she actually likes your persistence;
    keep persisting and soon all that you want will be yours.

Meanwhile, should she be borne reclining on well-cushioned litters,
    make sure that you approach casually (don't make a show).
Lest any man who's standing nearby should be ready to eavesdrop,
    shrewdly make your words cunning, ambiguous, sly.
Should she be idly walking within the broad portico's shadow,
    see that you linger there, sharing her leisurely stroll.
Sometimes try to precede her and sometimes follow behind her;
    sometimes quicken your step, sometimes slow to a crawl.

Don't be ashamed to bypass a few of the columns between you;
    don't be ashamed to join *your* side to *her* side, as well.
Don't let the beautiful creature sit down in the theater without you:
    over her shoulders she'll wear something worth a close look.
Fix your steady gaze on her beauty, sit and admire her.
    Eyebrows can say a lot; gestures express many thoughts.
Clap when a mime represents some lady fair in his dancing;
    cheer when actors portray lovers and amorous men.
Stand up whenever she stands up, and sit there as long as she's sitting;
    gladly waste your time just as your loved one suggests.

Only, I beg you, refrain from curling your hair with hot irons;
    don't use pumice to scrape hair off your legs, I advise.
Leave that to eunuchs who praise in howling Phrygian measures
    Mother Cybele, great daughter of Heaven and Earth.
Men look better when not so dandified, don't they? When Theseus
    stole Ariadne, no brooch lent its grace to his hair.
Never especially chic, Hippolytus gratified Phaedra;
    handsome Adonis pleased Venus, though bred in the woods.
Just make sure you're clean, let exercise tan your complexion;
    see that your toga fits, rid it of dirt and of stains.
Don't tie your shoe strap too tight, and wipe all the rust off the buckle;
    don't let a shoe that's too large make your feet seem to swim.
Don't let your wayward hair be ruined by amateur haircuts;
    always let practiced hands clip both your beard and your locks.
Don't let your nails grow too long, and never let them be dirty;
    don't let unsightly hairs thrust themselves out of your nose.
See that your breath is fresh, with no disagreeable odors;
    don't offend people's scent, smelling like sheep or like goats.
Leave all the rest for women of little virtue to practice,
    leave it to men who desire men as partners in bed.

Bacchus now calls to his bard; the wine god, also, aids lovers;
    gladly he pokes up those flames, burning himself first of all.
Over a beach unfamiliar to her, Cretan maid Ariadne
    madly roamed, where small Naxos is whipped by the waves:
just as she was, half-asleep, her tunic unbelted and open,

feet unshod and her blonde tresses completely undone,
calling to Theseus the grim over waters that never responded,
    tears that she didn't deserve washing her delicate cheeks.
Though she shouted and wept at the same time, still it became her;
    tears such as those don't make maidens look ugly at all.
Now once again her fists assail that softest of bosoms.
    "Traitor, you now depart; what's to become of me here?
What's to become of me here?" she cries; and suddenly cymbals
    ring out all over the shore, tambourines wildly resound.
Stricken with fear, she swooned and all further words were unspoken,
    not one drop of blood left in her body so pale.
Now the female attendants of Bacchus, their hair madly streaming,
    came with his satyrs swift: signs that the god would arrive.
Here he comes, that old drunkard Silenus—swaybacked his donkey.
    Riding unsurely, he grasps wildly at hairs of its mane.
After his Maenads he goes, while they now avoid, now attack him;
    on goes that rider unskilled, prodding his mount with a stick.
Slipping off the long-eared donkey, he hits the ground head first;
    all the satyrs shout: "Father, get up now, get up!"
Next comes the god himself, his chariot topped with a grapevine;
    harnessed to golden reins, tigers are drawing him on.
Now the girl had lost voice, color, remembrance of Theseus;
    thrice she attempted to flee, thrice she was held back by fear;
just as slender grain stalks, blown by the wind, start to shudder,
    so did she—like light rushes in waterlogged swamps.
"Here," said the god, "am I; you'll find me more faithful a lover.
    Cast aside your fear; Bacchus's bride you shall be.
Heaven shall be my bride gift; you'll now be a star in the heavens,
    now as the Cretan Crown guiding ships in distress."
Saying this, down he leapt from his chariot, lest his two tigers
    frighten her, and the sand yielded to feet planted there.
Clasping her now to his heart (the maiden could make no resistance),
    off he went with her: gods easily do what they want.
Some of the throng hymned Hymen, the god of marriage; some, Bacchus;
    thus on their hallowed bed god and bride coalesced.

★

Therefore, when Bacchus's blessings are openly set down before you,
    when some woman reclines partnering you on your couch,
pray to the Bacchus of nighttime and all holy beings nocturnal:
    "Don't make the wine I consume go too fast to my head!"
This is your chance to reveal many thoughts that you may have kept silent;
    let her think that each syllable's meant just for her.
Dip your finger in wine and trace words of love on the table,
    showing her that you now feel that her favors are yours.
Gaze in her eyes with eyes that clearly reveal all your passion;
    silent lips can possess eloquent words and a voice.
Be the first one to reach for the cup that the fair one has tasted;
    drink from the very spot sanctified by her sweet lips.
Where her fingers have dipped in the dish, whatever the food there,
    make it your business to dip, grazing her hand all the while.
Do all your best to win over the woman's husband and please him:
    once he's your friend, he's more useful to you than he was.
Should the sequence of drinking be ordered by lot, let him draw first;
    should your wreath fall from your head, give it to hubby to wear.
Should his place at the table be lower or equal, then let him
    take any food he wants first; *you* be the second to speak.
Tested and tried is the path of cheating by means of a friendship
    (though it's tested and tried, nevertheless it's a sin;
proxies can go too far, being more than innocent agents,
    wishing to supervise more than was left in their charge).

Limits must be observed in drinking, and now I'll expound them:
    never let head or feet fail in their usual tasks.
First and foremost, watch out for squabbles occasioned by boozing:
    don't let unruly hands force you into a fight.
Once, at a famed wedding feast men killed a stupid drunk centaur;
    food and wine go best paired with laughter and fun.
Sing if you own a good voice; if your arms are supple, do miming;
    should you possess any gifts, use them to pleasure the guests.
Actual drunkenness harms, but you'll raise a laugh if you fake it:
    let your tricky tongue stutter and stagger and reel.
All your actions and words too heedless of company manners—
    let them suggest one cause: wine too freely imbibed.

Say, "Good luck to this lady, and equal good luck to her bedmate,"
    secretly praying that ill luck will light on that man.
Then, when the tables are taken away and it's time for departure,
    means of approach you'll find handed to you by the crowd.
Join them and, mingling in, sidle up to the lady, who's leaving,
    pluck at her side with your hand, fondle her foot with your foot.
Now is the moment for talking; let no rural modesty stop you!
    Venus and Chance, as well, favor the man who is bold.
Please don't study your speeches, arranging your words like a poet:
    once you're determined to win, eloquence comes by itself.
Just play a lover's part, let your words suggest that you're wounded;
    use any ploy to inspire trust in the feelings you claim.
This won't be hard to achieve; every woman believes she's a siren:
    ugly as sin though she be, still she'll be proud of her looks.
Frequently, though, a vile deceiver begins to feel true love,
    often becoming a real lover, although he had feigned.
Therefore, ladies, be all the more openminded toward feigners:
    sometimes love that's false suddenly proves to be true.
Now is the time to catch her mind off guard with your blarney,
    just as a flowing stream eats away at its banks.
Don't be too lazy to heap your praise on her face or her hairdo;
    laud her fingers so slim, laud those daintiest feet.
Hearing their beauty praised gives great delight to the chastest;
    virgins, too, derive joy from concern with their charms.
Why are Minerva and Juno ashamed even now because Paris
    once in the Trojan woods failed to award them the prize?
Juno's bird, the peacock, displays its plumes when you praise them;
    fail to praise those plumes: peacocks will hide them away.
Horses, too, between their rounds of chariot racing
    love to have their manes combed, love pats on their neck.

Don't lag behind in your promising; promises gull every woman;
    swear by what gods you will: keep on making those vows.
Jupiter, up in his heaven, smiling at lies told by lovers,
    orders blustery winds boldly to blow them away.
That same god was accustomed to swear oaths falsely to Juno,
    calling on Styx; he now likes the example he set.

Trusting in gods is handy and, since it's handy, let's do so;
    let their altars of yore still receive incense and wine.
Nor are they ever restrained by carefree, slumberlike stupor.
    Live uprightly; you see, gods are watching your deeds.
Give back things that you've borrowed, always stick to your duty,
    practice no fraud, have hands guiltless of murder and theft.
Wise men keep out of trouble by cheating no one but women;
    save for that fraud alone, trustworthy always they stay.
Cheat a cheater! You'll find that cheaters are criminal people
    mostly; let every net laid by them snare only them.
Legend tells the Egyptians once sorely longed for the rainfall
    needed by crops; for nine years drought had ravaged their fields.
Then their king Busiris, informed by a prophet from Cyprus
    Jove could be appeased solely by foreigners' blood,
ordered the prophet who gave that advice to be the first victim:
    "Egypt shall have its rain thanks to your blood from abroad."
Phalaris, tyrant in Sicily, roasted the limbs of Perillus,
    testing the bull of bronze made by that man of bad luck.
Both those monarchs were right: it's justice without any equal
    seeing artists of doom dying by works of their own.
Thus, if a woman's lies are deservedly countered by new lies,
    that's the example she set punishing *her* in her turn.

Also, it's useful to weep, for tears can melt away diamonds;
    let her see, if you can, cheeks that are constantly wet.
Since you can't guarantee that tears will come at your bidding,
    should they fail, touch your two eyes with hands that are damp.
What wise man wouldn't mingle a heartfelt kiss with his soft words?
    (No return? Then pretend kisses not granted were real.)
Maybe she'll struggle at first and loudly call you a lowlife;
    while she struggles she'll still wish she were losing the match.
Only, don't kiss her too roughly, lest those soft lips should be injured;
    make sure she can't complain saying your play was too gross.
One who has stolen some kisses and won't steal others deserves to
    lose them all (I include those he already has got!).
After the kisses, I ask, what was lacking to make you quite blissful?
    Shame didn't stand in your way: countrified clumsiness did!

Don't be afraid to use force; force flatters women, they like it;
    often they want to appear hostile, but give what you want.
She who succumbs to surprise attacks in that amorous warfare
    gloats on them, takes them to be gifts she receives, and not crimes.
She who might have been forced, but escaped without any struggle,
    feels sad, though her face simulates feelings of joy.
Phoebe and sister Hilaria were kidnapped by Castor and Pollux,
    yet each kidnapper proved pleasing to each kidnappee.
Though it's an oft-told tale, it well repays a retelling,
    how Achilles and sweet Deidamia were linked.
Venus had handed over the prize for her victory (Helen)
    after defeating those two goddesses outside of Troy.
Priam's new daughter-in-law had already arrived from her country,
    married in Greece, but now living in Paris's home.
All the Greeks now swore they'd support the put-upon husband;
    one man's sorrow became everyone's thorn in the side.
Had he not been obeying his mother's orders, Achilles
    might have looked cowardly dressed head to foot just like a girl
there on the isle of Skyros. Achilles, why trifle with weaving?
    Out of Minerva's arts that's not the one meant for you!
What are you doing with baskets? Your hands are more fit for a buckler:
    why should those man-slaying hands hold onto skeins of soft wool?
Throw away all those twisted threads and effeminate spindles!
    Let's see Thessaly's spears brandished by hands such as yours!
That same chamber, by chance, then sheltered the princess of Skyros;
    when he seduced her, she knew one of her handmaids was male.
Yes, she was taken by force, the story would have us believe so;
    yet she was very content having been taken that way.
Often she called out "Remain!" to the quickly departing Achilles
    after he cast away distaffs for armor and arms.
What of his violent ways? Why urge him to stay, why cajole him,
    Deidamia, now? Didn't he take you by force?
Truly, it sometimes brings shame to initiate loving adventures;
    yet, when someone else starts them, it's fun to submit.
Take it from me, a young man is trusting too much to his good looks
    should he really expect women to make the first move.
Let the man be the first to accost her with words of entreaty,

let her kindly receive prayers he addresses to her.
Ask if she'll deign to be yours; she's merely awaiting that question.
    Tell her the cause of your love, tell how your longing began.
Jove, in the days of yore, romanced those heroines, begged them;
    never was Jove himself pleaded with, wooed, or seduced.
Still, if you find your pleas inflating her haughtiness merely,
    let the enterprise go, quickly retracing your steps.
Many a woman desires what she loses, yet hates the insistent;
    never push matters too far, making her weary of you.
Men who plead shouldn't always announce their hopes of a conquest;
    feigning to be just a friend, bring love covertly in.
This approach (I've seen it) has won the severest ones over;
    just an admirer before, now you have got her in bed.

Pale complexions are wrong for sailors; they ought to be swarthy,
    thanks to the waves of the sea, thanks to the rays of the sun.
Such a complexion is shameful to farmers, who constantly churn up
    earth in the great outdoors using a harrow or plow.
Thus, you athletes, too, contending for garlands of olive,
    you, too, would shrink with shame should your bodies be pale.
Lovers, though, ought to look white, the proper hue for a lover;
    that is the hue to possess; fools, only, think it won't count.
Giant Orion was pale when he roamed the woods, losing Side;
    shepherd boy Daphnis was pale, spurned by the nymph he adored.
Waste away, proving thereby that you love her! Don't think it shameful
    covering up your neat hair with a shadowing hood.
Nights of insomnia slowly slenderize bodies of lovers;
    so does their terrible grief; so does anxiety, too.
Want to obtain your desires? Then look like a woebegone misfit;
    everyone seeing you cries: "*There* goes a man who's in love!"
Should I lament, or remind you that right and wrong are all mixed up?
    Friendship is only a word, trustingness merely a joke.
Men are never safe when they praise their girls to a buddy;
    once he believes your praise, there he is, taking your place.
Tell me Achilles's bed was never besmirched by Patroclus;
    tell me Pirithous, too, never loved Theseus's wife.
Pylades toward the spouse of his friend Orestes was never

more than a brother, just like Castor to Helen of Troy.
Should you expect the same, it's just like hoping that apples
    grow on a tamarisk bush, honey seep from a stream.
Only what's shameful is pleasing; men long for mere gratification;
    should it provide *them* with fun, let all the others feel pain!
What a state of affairs! No enemies threaten a lover;
    those he thinks are true—let him shun *them* to be safe!
Watch out for brothers and longtime friends and cherished relations;
    they are the ones you should fear, *they* are your actual foes.

Well, I thought I was done, but since women's hearts are so varied,
    use a thousand ploys, one for each woman you crave.
Not all products are grown in the same soil: some is for vineyards,
    some bears olive trees, some is well suited to wheat.
Hearts have as many trends as the human face has expressions;
    wise men adapt themselves quickly to differing ways,
just as changeable Proteus now trickles away into water,
    now turns into a tree, lion, or bristle-clad boar.
Some fish have to be speared, while others snap at the fishhook;
    some are lured into nets hauled by tightly drawn ropes.
Likewise, don't use *one* approach for every age; elderly roedeer
    stand further back when they see snares that are laid for their sake.
Act like scholars with stupid women, like rogues with the prudish:
    soon they'll pity themselves, all their self-confidence gone.
That's how women, afraid to trust the most upright of lovers,
    fall, with a loss of face, right into lesser men's arms.

Now Book One is concluded, but more advice is still coming.
    Here for a while my boat, anchored securely, will rest.

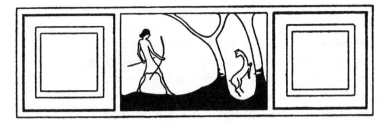

BOOK TWO

Shout triumphantly, shout exultantly, over and over!
    Quarry I hunted has now fallen right into my net.
Joyously lovers, my pupils, all crown my verses with palm leaves,
    finding they far surpass Hesiod's or Homer's attempts.
That's how Paris felt when sailing from warloving Sparta,
    spreading his radiant white sails with Helen on board.
That's how Pelops felt, who, winning her hand in the race, bore
    Hippodamia away riding his chariot swift.
Young men, what's your hurry? Our ship is still in mid-ocean;
    far is the port I seek, still we must sail to our goal.
I'm not satisfied merely because my words won your sweetheart;
    my skill captured her, *my* skill must now make her stay.
No less work is needed to keep something after you've found it:
    chance may affect the quest, now art comes into play.
Venus and Cupid, if ever you favored me, now is the time to:
    Erato, too, lyric Muse (Eros lurks in your name).
Great are my plans: to disclose the arts by which Love is made steadfast,
    though that roving boy wanders all over the world.
Also, he *can* be elusive, he's got two wings to escape with;
    never an easy task, tying those runaways down!

Minos, king of Crete, blocked every available exit;
    Daedalus nevertheless fled him on wings that he made.
After he built the maze to enclose that lewd mother's offspring,
    Minotaur (half man, also partly a bull),
Daedalus turned to Minos and asked for an end to his exile;

"Justest of men, let my own native land harbor my urn!
Though I was harried by hostile fates, and therefore I couldn't
   live in the land of my birth, there at least let me die.
Let my son go home, if you feel I'd be wrongly rewarded;
   should you be against sparing the boy, then spare *me*."
All of this he spoke. But much more might he have spoken;
   still the stubborn king never allowed him to leave.
Once he acknowledged this, the inventor spoke to himself thus:
   "Daedalus, now you must use every trick up your sleeve.
Minos retains control of the land and control of the ocean;
   neither soil nor sea aids you in running away.
Only a trail through the sky can save you: take to the sky, then.
   Jupiter up above, pardon my impudent plan!
No, it's not part of my scheme to visit your star-studded dwelling;
   only, I can escape Minos by no other route.
Show me a way across Styx, the underworld river: I'll swim it!
   Brand-new laws must be framed, fitting my novel approach."
Difficulties sharpen the wits, for who would believe that
   men could choose a path pointing into the skies?
Now he sets in array the birds' mode of steering (their feathers),
   strengthening that very light tissue with tight bands of cloth,
binding the lower part with melted wax—and imagine!—
   now he had fashioned a new work to attest to his skill.
Beaming all over, his son young Icarus waxed every feather,
   all unaware that his own shoulders would carry the load.
"These are the keels," said his father, "prepared to take us back home, son;
   this is the way by which Minos will be overruled.
Minos had barred every exit—the sky he was forced to leave open.
   Skies are accessible: fly fearlessly forth on my craft!
Only, don't stare at the stars of the Bear or her neighbor Boötes,
   nor at Orion the great, wielding that terrible sword;
follow *me* on the wings I have given you. *I* shall precede you;
   your only job is to come next; follow *me* and you're safe.
Soaring too near the sun, you see, on our heavenly journey,
   might make all the wax melt away in its heat.
Should we graze the sea too closely on low-flying plumage,
   every feather would lose buoyancy, splashed by the waves.

Hold your course in between, and keep alert to the wind, too;
   heed where the breezes head, following *them* on your wings."
Handing out this advice, he adjusts the wings on the boy, then
   teaches him their use, just like a mothering bird.
Next he straps the wings he created onto his shoulders,
   poising his body to fly (timidly: this was so new!).
Now, all set for the takeoff, he kissed his juvenile offspring;
   tears flowed down his cheeks, tears he couldn't hold back.
Not as high as a mountain; a hill arose from the lowland;
   that was the place where the two launched themselves into the air.
Daedalus, flapping his own wings, kept glancing back at his son's wings,
   steadily keeping the course meant to insure his escape.
Now they both are charmed by that newly found locomotion;
   Icarus grows too bold, flying too bravely to last.
One man, fishing with flexible rod, just happened to spot them;
   down fell that man's right hand, heedless of previous tasks.
Now they had passed, on their left, the islands of Samos and Naxos,
   Paros, and Delos as well (isle that Apollo adores).
On their right Lebinthos lay, and woody Calymne,
   Astypalaea, too, blessed with abundance of fish.
Then the lad, too rash and youthfully casting off caution,
   headed too high, no more following Father's advice.
Now the tight bindings grow loose, the wax melts away in the sunshine;
   arms, now flapping in vain, lose their support from the breeze.
Frightened, from up in the sky he stared at the waters beneath him;
   dark night covered those eyes stricken with horrible fear.
Now all the wax is gone; the arms he is waving are bare now.
   Shivering, now he finds nothing to help keep him up.
Plummeting, loudly he cries: "Oh, father, father, I'm sinking!"
   While he was speaking, green waters closed over his lips.
Then the unhappy father, a father no more, called his name out:
   "Icarus, where are you now, flying under which pole?
Icarus!" still he cried, then he saw the boy's plumes in the ocean.
   Earth now covers his bones; local waves bear his name.

Minos hadn't the power to keep human beings from flying;
   yet, as part of my plan, *I* shall restrain the winged god.

No use trying Thessalian arts and relying on magic,
   potions derived from a growth ripped from the head of a foal.
All of Medea's herbs are useless to make love enduring;
   so are the magical spells Marsians chant in their hills.
Jason would still belong to Medea, Ulysses to Circe,
   thanks to their arts, were spells able to stabilize love.
Don't expect pale philters to work on the women you care for;
   philters can damage their minds, leading them on to go mad.
Never use methods unrighteous; be lovable, then they will love you.
   Not good figures, not good faces alone do the trick.
Though you're handsome as Nireus, that chief so vaunted by Homer,
   handsome as Hylas, the youth raped by sex-crazy nymphs,
still, to hold onto your woman, avoiding the shock of rejection,
   let intellectual gifts join with your bodily ones.
Handsomeness, always a weak thing, dwindles away as time passes;
   years that slowly plod on steadily wear it away.
Violets aren't always in blossom, nor wide-gaping lilies;
   roses, too, fall away, leaving behind only thorns.
One day, good-looking lad, you'll find gray hairs in your hairbrush;
   wrinkles will follow in turn, plowing that beautiful face.
Now is the time to fashion a mind that will outlive your beauty;
   only your mind will last down to the day of your death.
Don't think it needless to cultivate arts of civilization;
   practice the two classic tongues, learning both Latin and Greek.
No great shakes for looks was Ulysses; how he could speak, though!
   How he inflamed two sea goddesses with his appeal!
Ah, how often Calypso grieved at his plans for departure,
   telling him that the seas wouldn't submit to his oars!
How she begged him to tell her his Troy tale over and over,
   forcing him to employ different wording each time!
There they stood on the shore, and there the lovely Calypso
   urged him to tell her the dire fate of King Rhesus of Thrace.
Deep in the sands of the beach with his lightweight staff (for he bore one)
   mighty Ulysses drew pictures of stories he told.
"Here," he'd say, "is Troy" (after building walls at the seashore),
   here the stream Simois; here, imagine my camp.
Here is the plain" (and he draws a plain) "which our slaughter of Dolon

stained when, one night, he set out after Thessalian steeds.
These are the tents of Rhesus the Thracian, Sithonia's ruler;
   that very night I rode back with the horses I stole."
Many an exploit he drew there, when, suddenly, waves from the ocean
   washed away Troy and washed Rhesus away with his camp.
Then the goddess said, "Those waters you trust for your voyage—
   don't you see what feats, what great names they've destroyed?"

Therefore, don't trust too much in good looks that will later desert you;
   furthermore, you must possess something more solid than looks.
Skillfully managed compassion is best for winning folks over;
   harshness leads to hate, causing merciless wars.
Hawks are hateful to us, for they live by always attacking;
   wolves, too, because they're found feeding on timorous sheep.
Swallows, though, are never our victims, being so gentle,
   while for doves we provide towers to live in, as well.
Far from me may quarrels remain and contentions of sharp tongues!
   Love is soft, it demands nurture through sweetness of speech.
Let wives drive their husbands away by grumbling, let husbands
   drive away wives; let them deem couples are always at war.
Wives must be like that; quarrels are normal parts of their dowry.
   Mistresses, though, ought to hear nothing but welcoming words.
Not by some legal decree did you and she end up in *one* bed;
   love is law for you two, armed with legitimate rights.
Seeing your loved one again, bring words of pleasure and solace;
   that way, each visit of yours makes it a red-letter day.
Nor are these lessons in love that I offer meant for the wealthy:
   men who can give rich gifts don't have need of my art.
Men who make presents whenever they please are sufficiently clever;
   they can take over my job, *their* way is surer than mine.
I am the poor man's poet, because I was poor when romancing;
   gifts were out of my reach, *I* was dependent on words.
Poor men need to be careful as lovers; they can't be insulting.
   Poor men put up with a lot rich men never would stand.
Once, I recall, I was angry and mussed up my mistress's hairdo;
   one fit of wrath, and I lost God knows how many days!
Nor do I think that I tore her robe, as she later insisted;

nevertheless, its cost came out of *my* pocket, too.
Men, if you're clever, avoid the sins of this penitent teacher;
    don't incur the expense caused by an act that's inept.
Fight with the Parthian hordes, keep peace with a woman who's well bred;
    frolic with her, and enjoy all of the raptures of love.

Should she be less than kind, should she fail to treat you politely,
    stand your ground, persist; some day she'll surely repent.
Crooked boughs detached from trees will bend if you're patient;
    should you apply too much force, those branches would snap.
Calm, adaptable patience swims waters: you can't cross a river
    swimming against its flow, thwarting its current in vain.
Patient submission tames tigers, subdues North African lions,
    makes the ox at last bow its neck to the yoke.
Who was ever less pliant than Arcadian-born Atalanta?
    Nevertheless, that shrew yielded to masculine feats.
Young Milanion often (so goes the story) bewailed her
    spite and his own hard fate, sighing under the trees.
Often he lugged her snares, obeying behests of the huntress;
    often he killed grim boars, spitting them just for her sake.
Wounded was he with arrows shot by a centaur, his rival,
    yet a more famous bow, Cupid's, hurt him much worse.
You need not pick up a bow and scale Arcadian woodlands,
    you've no occasion to bear nets and snares on your neck.
Don't go exposing your breast to deadly enemy arrows;
    cautious men will find easy the orders I give.
Should she resist, give in; you'll gain the victory yielding;
    make sure you act out all roles that the lady assigns.
Should she cast blame, cast blame; whatever she fancies, approve it;
    sanction whatever she says, whether it's yes or it's no.
Should she laugh, do the same; remember to weep if she's weeping;
    let your face reflect moods dictated by her.
Should she be playing games, casting ivory dice when her turn comes,
    see that you make bad throws, see that you make a wrong move.
Playing together with larger dice? If she loses, give her no forfeit;
    make sure luckless throws fall to your lot every time.
Should the piece that you move be a "little robber" in *that* game,

let your warrior fall victim to foes made of glass.
You yourself hold over her her parasol outstretched and open!
    You yourself disperse crowds and give her more room!
Should she desire her well-wrought couch, be there with a footstool!
    Take her slippers off; later, put them back on.
Though you're shivering, too, when your lady's cold you must place her
    hand on your own manly chest, giving her comfort and warmth.
Never think it beneath you (it *may* be, but surely she'll like it):
    let your freeborn hand hold up a mirror for her!
Hercules held up the heaven to which he was later entitled,
    after he'd slain each fierce monster that Juno had sent;
later in life he's said to have held up a basket of woolwork,
    spinning among the girls down by Ionian shores.
That Tirynthian hero obeyed a woman's commandments:
    you think that you can avoid doing exactly the same?
Bidden to go to the Forum to meet her, get there too early
    each and every time; don't depart till it's late.
Any appointment she gives you, drop everything else and show up there!
    Run! Don't let any crowd stop you from keeping the date!
After a dinner party at night she's hastening homeward:
    summoned by her, submit readily, act as her slave!
Off in her villa, she sends for you; love despises the lazy.
    No conveyance at hand? Foot it, and slog all the way!
What if the day is hot and you're thirsty, baked by the Dog Star?
    What if the drifting snow makes every thoroughfare white?

Love is a sort of war, and sluggish men have no place there;
    guarding its banners is *not* work for the timid or shy.
Night and tempest and long, long trails and terrible hardships,
    labors of every kind lurk in that amorous camp.
Often you'll suffer from rain that's released by the clouds up in heaven,
    often you'll suffer from cold, lying on ground that is bare.
Legend tells that Apollo once guarded the herds of Admetus,
    hiding his glory away down in some miserable hut.
Good enough for Apollo, but not for you? Don't be prideful!
    Show that you crave a love calculated to last.
Maybe the road you travel is never a safe or a smooth one;

maybe you'll find every door closed with an obstinate bolt.
That's the case? Slip headlong right into the house by the skylight!
  Let its high windows provide secret ways to get in!
Thus you'll make her happy, she'll know *she* occasioned your perils;
  yes, she'll be grateful for such tokens of genuine love!
Often Leander was minded to miss a meeting with Hero;
  still, he swam that strait, hoping she'd notice he cared.

Curry favor with ranking handmaids (don't be ashamed to),
  don't be ashamed to be seen currying favor with slaves.
Greet each servant by name, you'll find that it always repays you;
  truly ambitious men take even slaves by the hand.
Should they ask it (it's no great expense), well, give them a little
  gift on Good Fortune Day; any small trinket will do.
Also make presents to maids on July the seventh, when handmaids,
  dressed as matronly brides, fooled the gullible Gauls.
Trust me, win over the commons, for doorkeepers always are plain folk,
  also the man who lies guarding the door to her room.
Nor do I ask you to make rich presents to women you sigh for;
  let them be gifts, though small, chosen with elegant taste.
While your fields are bearing, your orchards laden with rich fruit,
  let some slave bring her tithes, baskets of countryside goods.
Say they were sent to you here from your great estate in the suburbs,
  even though they were bought, fetched from some market in Rome.
Let it be grapes that he brings, or let it be chestnuts, once loved by
  Vergil's shepherdess, though "now she loves them no more."
Send her a thrush or a pigeon; each bird is sure to bear witness
  you're still mindful of *her*, *she's* still queen of your heart.
Shameful it is when such gifts bring hopes of death and of barren
  old age; go to hell, you who bear criminal gifts!

Why do I need to remind you? Send amorous poetry, also!
  hear me sighing, "Alas!"—verse isn't highly esteemed.
People praise it, it's true, but what they want is rich presents;
  let them be wealthy enough, even barbarians please.
This is the Golden Age, of a certainty; gold buys you honors,
  gold is the firmest link joining affectionate hearts.

Homer, pay us a visit and bring along all of the Muses!
    Homer, without a gift, trust me: we'll show you the door!
True, a few ladies are learned and cultured (they're the exception).
    Most don't know a damn thing; still, they try to be smart.
Praise both groups in your verse; whether good or less good, recite it
    winningly, lovingly, well; sweet be the sound of your voice.
Poems you've stayed awake writing, both groups may appreciate greatly,
    finding them, maybe, to be tiny gifts that you've made.

Things you would do for your own sake, things that you know will be useful,
    see to it that they're things always requested by *her*.
Maybe you've promised one of your slaves that you'll give him his freedom;
    let him pretend it's a great favor coming from *her*.
Maybe you've spared a slave from punishment, spared him from shackles;
    let those kindly acts seem to be owing to *her*.
Let the advantage be yours, but give your sweetheart the credit;
    nothing is lost and she's glad, playing the bountiful role.
This above all, you men who want to hold onto your mistress:
    make her believe that her charm smites you and holds you in awe.
When she's in Tyrian robes, say Tyrian robes are the finest;
    should she war Coan garb, say that there's no place like Cos.
Is she clad in gold? Say gold bricks are hardly more precious.
    Wool is adorning her frame? Sing all the praises of wool.
Should she be dressed in only a slip, cry out: "You ignite me!"
    Yet, with a timid voice say you're afraid she'll catch cold.
Has she arranged her hair with a part in it? Praise for her hairdo!
    Has she curled it with hot irons? Praise for her curls!
Gape at her arms when she's dancing, thrill to her voice when she's singing;
    then, when her number is done, shout out: "Encore! Don't stop!"
Make the most of your hours of intercourse, show her your pleasure;
    moaning aloud, let her know just how she sets you aflame.
Even if normally violent, normally grim as Medusa,
    then she'll be soft as silk, gentle and meek with her lad.
Just make sure your words don't reveal that you're only pretending;
    don't let your features spoil any impression you're made.
Guile works best when it's hidden; discovered, it's liable to shame you.
    Through your own fault, you'll have lost all your credit for good.

★

Often, on autumn days, when the year is reaching its zenith,
    days when the purple wine swells each ripening grape,
now we're assailed by cold, next minute we're all hot and sweaty;
    changeable weather will make bodies languid and weak.
Here's to your sweetheart's good health! But should she fall ill and be ailing,
    finding the very sky causing her sickness and pain,
then let her be well aware of all your loving compassion;
    sow the seeds of a rich crop you'll be happy to reap.
Feel no repugnance to follow the gloomy course of her illness;
    let your hands perform anything *she* may request.
Let her see you weep; be constantly giving her kisses;
    let her bone-dry lips drink the tears that you shed.
Wish her well time and again, out loud; whenever you want to,
    say you've had happy dreams, dreams you can tell her about.
Bring some old woman in who knows how to purify sickrooms;
    let her tremulous hands carry in sulfur and eggs.
All of this will bespeak your loving concern for your mistress;
    this is a path that has led often to grateful bequests.
Meanwhile, take great care that your services never offend her;
    yes, be obliging, but set limits to all you perform.
Never forbid her the dishes she likes, or offer her bitter
    drafts; let your rival mix horrid medicinal brews.

Winds that billowed your sails when you first set out from the seacoast
    shouldn't be still counted on, once you are out on the main.
Youthfully aimless love must grow firm with maturer reflections;
    nurture your passion well; strengthen it, giving it time.
Now you're afraid of the bull that you used to stroke in its calf days;
    now you lie under a tree once a sapling and frail.
Rivers are small at their source; flowing on, they get fuller and fuller,
    all along their course swelling with incoming streams.
See that your mistress gets used to you: nothing is stronger than custom;
    till you've attained that end, never grow weary or flag.
Always be there in her sight, let your voice always ring in her hearing;
    every night, every day, let her examine your face.
After your confidence grows and you're sure she'll miss you when absent,
    sure that she's likely to fret finding you *so* far away,

give her a rest; plowed fields reward you once they've lain fallow;
    earth that's parched soaks up rain when it falls from the sky.
Theseus' son Demophoon, left Phyllis cold with his presence;
    once he had sailed away, Phyllis ignited with flame.
Absence of husband Ulysses made sweet Penelope suffer;
    Protesilaus away, Laodamia repined.
Don't be gone too long, though, for length of time makes them forget you;
    absentee love won't last; new lovers come on the scene.
Far from home, Menelaus left Helen too lonely in Sparta;
    Helen found solace at night, cozy in Paris's arms.
How could you be so dumb, Menelaus? After you left them,
    wife and guest were both under one roof, and alone.
Why did you so insanely entrust your dove to a goshawk?
    Would you entrust a full sheepfold to ravening wolves?
No fault of Helen's was that; the adulterer's not guilty, either:
    merely, what *you* would have done (anyone would have), he did.
You're to blame for their sin; you gave them the place and occasion;
    that poor wife only took counsel that *you* had supplied.
What could she do with her husband away and a stud in the guestroom?
    Wouldn't she feel afraid, sleeping alone in your bed?
Let Menelaus say what he likes; I exonerate Helen;
    Helen just seized her chance, finding her guest so humane.

Ruddy boars at the height of their fury aren't so savage,
    tumbling a whole pack of mad hounds with a flash of their tusks;
female lions, when suckling their cubs, are never so vicious;
    nor is the tiny asp, trodden ineptly, so wild:
no, a *woman's* more fierce when she finds herself ousted by rivals:
    flames flaring up in her face point to the state of her mind.
Into a fire she'd dart, or onto a sword; all decorum
    set aside, she would seem smitten by Bacchus's horns.
Savage Medea avenged her wrongs, her betrayal by Jason,
    killing her own two sons (that's how foreigners act!).
Procne turned into a swallow when slaying her boy to get vengeance;
    look at the bird and you'll see bloodstains all over its breast.
Playing the field will break up affairs that seem well knit and solid;
    prudent men should avoid letting such mishaps occur.

Still, this decree of mine isn't meant to tie you to *one* love.
    God forbid! Even young brides can't pin you down if you roam.
Have your fun, but in secret, and never allude to your mischief:
    never strut or brag, never boast of your sins.
Don't give gifts to another love that your first one may hear of;
    don't have any new trysts slated for regular hours.
Lest your earlier sweetheart detect your romance's location,
    make sure to hold each new date in a separate spot.
Writing letters on wax, take care, look all over the tablets;
    don't let your old love find traces of notes to the new.
Venus, offended, will wage fair wars and hurl back your missiles;
    you made her weep in the past; *she'll* do the same thing to you.
While Agamemnon was fully contented with Clytemnestra, his wife, too,
    kept her chastity; *he* set new examples for her.
Chryses, the priest, she'd heard, that bearer of fillets and laurel,
    couldn't make the Greek chief let his daughter depart.
No, Agamemnon made off with Briseis, who wept when abducted
    (thus, Achilles's wrath lengthened the course of the war).
This she had only heard, but her own eyes looked on Cassandra,
    booty of war brought home, dear to her great captor's heart.
Then she welcomed Aegisthus to vengeful bosom and bedroom,
    slew Agamemnon, as well, wrathful because of his crimes.

Should your amours be revealed though you've done your best to conceal them,
    keep on denying them flat, even if clear as the day.
Don't be more humble than usual, don't be too openly coaxing:
    actions like these are too patent tokens of guilt.
Then, don't spare your loins; your peace is dependent on *one* thing:
    wipe out all her complaints, starting an orgy of sex.
Some recommend taking savory (harmful herb, in my judgment);
    I don't counsel it; that's poison, take it from me.
Some mix peppercorns with seeds of the nettles that sting you;
    some use chrysanthemum heads ground up in old vintage wine.
Venus, however, the goddess of Eryx in Sicily's mountains,
    can't be compelled that way, yielding to magical might.
Eat, instead, white onions from Megara, home of Achaeans;
    eat aphrodisiac herbs (rocket, right out of your yard).

Gobble a lot of eggs, and honey straight from Hymettus,
    strengthen your organs with seeds bristly pine trees provide.

Learned Muse of mine, why deflect your path into magic?
    No, my chariot wheels! Graze a more meaningful post!
All you men who were just concealing your mischief, as ordered,
    change your course! I now counsel: own up to your sins!
Don't blame my flightiness, men: a round-keeled ship doesn't always
    carry its passenger load holding *one* wind in its sails.
Now it's a wind from the north we sail by, now it's an east wind;
    often a wind from the west puffs our sails, or the south.
Watch how a chariot driver now lets the reins dangle slackly,
    now with the greatest skill slows the impetuous steeds.
Some women thrive on rivals and rivalry: when you're too constant,
    they don't reciprocate, no; rivalry sharpens their love.
Things all going too well for her? Watch her get on her high horse!
    Equanimity flees, good luck drives it away.
Often a feeble fire, when its strength ebbs little by little,
    dwindles away and leaves ashes alone where it burned:
just add sulfur, and see its flames grow higher and higher;
    light that was shed before now is blazing anew.
Thus, when hearts get rusty from being too lazy and carefree,
    love needs a stimulus, love needs to be prodded with goads.
Make her feel insecure about you, heat up her lukewarm
    feelings, let her turn pale hearing that you've misbehaved.
Oh, how happy a man is, a million times over and then some,
    having a woman weep over a grief that he's caused!
Right after word of his crime has come to her ears (with reluctance),
    see that poor woman swoon, losing her color and voice!
Gods, let me be the one whose hair she rabidly pulls then!
    Let me be he whose cheeks then get viciously scratched!
Let her look at me tearfully, casting glances of menace,
    feeling, against her will, life without me would be void.
Let it not last too long if you grant her time to reproach you;
    don't let her wrath increase, heightened by lengthy delays.
Now is the moment to hold her snow-white neck in embraces,
    now let your loved one weep joyful tears on your breast.

Kiss her tears all away; give the weeper the pleasures of Venus.
　　Make your peace; only thus anger is conquered and flees.
After she's worn herself out with raging, you and your foe should
　　strike a treaty; have sex, then she'll be gentle again.
Concord, that goddess, will dwell with both, all weapons relinquished;
　　trust me, the Graces prefer living in peaceful abodes.
Doves that were recently squabbling now join their beaks in contentment,
　　trading words of love, words of joy, as they coo.

First, when the world began, all things were in aimless confusion,
　　no distinction between stars or the land or the sea;
soon the sky loomed over the land, which had sea for a girdle;
　　empty chaos withdrew, seeking its specified place.
Woods got beasts to inhabit them, air received birdlife.
　　Everywhere waters became filled with bevies of fish.
People, those days, just roamed the lonely fields, and possessed then
　　nothing but savage strength, bodies coarse and unkempt.
Forests provided their home; their food was grass, and their bedsteads
　　leaves; for a long, long time no one knew anyone else.
Love reputedly softened their savage spirits; their sex drive
　　made one woman, one man, halt in the very same place.
No one was there to teach them the way to attain their enjoyment;
　　Venus alone, and no art, saw that the needful was done.
Every bird has a mate to love, and partners for pleasure
　　female fish, when aroused, find in the midst of the sea.
Does submit to the stags, and serpents couple with serpents;
　　hounds and bitches, both, live for illicit amours.
Ewes are mounted by rams with joy, bulls service the heifer,
　　snubnosed nanny goats love dirty billy goats, too!
Mares turn to furies in love and hotly follow the stallions
　　over extensive terrain, even with rivers to cross.
Men: give angry women strong medicinal doses;
　　those alone can bring closure to festering grief.
Cures I have mentioned surpass the potions of Doctor Machaon,
　　chief physician at Troy; *they* will restore you to grace.

★

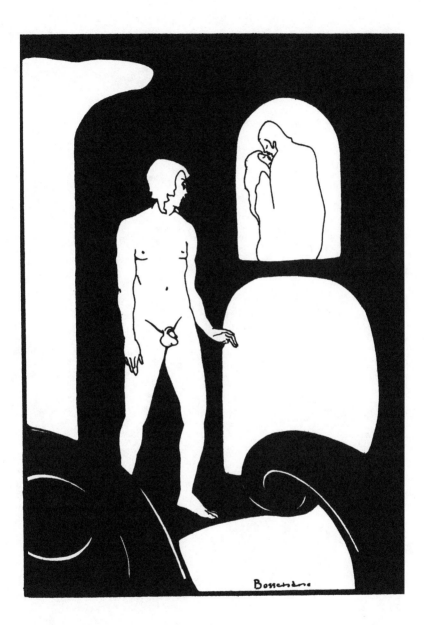

While I was singing those lines, all at once Apollo, appearing,
   struck the strings of his gold lyre with his musical thumb.
Laurels he held in his hand, and laurels covered the hallowed
   hairs of his head; he approached, poet right down to his toes.
"Teacher of lawless love," Apollo said to me gravely,
   "lead your disciples to *my* temple in Delphi; all come!
There there's a posted sign with a famous, world-renowned slogan,
   ordering every man: 'Know thy self first of all!'
Only a man with self-knowledge can act as a capable lover,
   carrying out his tasks wisely with all of his might.
Men to whom nature has given a nice face, let them be gazed on;
   men with good skin should leave one shoulder bare when they rest.
Men with the gift of the gab should shatter a taciturn silence.
   Sing if you do it well; drink if you know the right way.
Yet, good speakers should *not* declaim while people are talking,
   nor is that the time poets should spout their mad verse!"
Such was Apollo's decree, and I hope you all will obey him;
   place your trust in those deep, sacred words of the god.

Worldlier topics now claim me. The man who loves wisely will win, he'll
   reach the goal he seeks, practicing skills I profess.
Furrows don't always return any interest once they are seeded,
   nor will a favoring breeze rescue each floundering ship.
Things that can help out lovers are few, many more things will pain them;
   let them expect that great burdens will have to be borne.
Count up the hares on Mount Athos, the bees that forage on Hybla,
   count up the olives the gray trees of Minerva produce,
count up the shells on the seashore; *that's* how many woes love holds!
   Cupid's arrows drip densely with venom and gall.
Sometimes you're told she's gone out, but you chance to see her within doors.
   Seem to believe that she's out! Think that your eyes played a trick!
Nights of rendezvous come and you find her door locked up and bolted:
   bear up, and lay your frame down on the dirty, cold ground.
Sometimes a maid of hers, a liar with haughty demeanor,
   wonders out loud why a lout's always besieging the door.
Whimper, beseech that door, implore the hardhearted handmaid;
   take off your rosy wreath, hang it up on the jamb.

Times when she wants you to, visit her; other times, go away swiftly;
    freeborn men must avoid risks of becoming a bore.
Why should your mistress say, with good reason, "I just can't escape him"?
    Common sense never hurts, often it's even a help.
Don't find it shameful to hear your cherished mistress abuse you;
    let her hit you and, yes, kiss her delicate feet.

Why do I dwell on such details? My mind is on higher adventures.
    Lofty shall be my theme! Populace, pay me close heed.
Arduous is my plan, but arduous feats prove one's merit;
    toil, unremitting toil, such does my calling demand.
Put up calmly with rivals, and gain the ultimate triumph!
    Like some great consul, *you'll* stand on the Capitoline.
Think of it as not me, but oracular oaks in Dodona
    telling you this; it's the high summit of all of my art.
Seeing her signal another man, bear it! And don't touch her love notes;
    let her come whence she wants, let her go whither she likes.
Husbands allow this freedom to spouses they've legally married
    after consoling sleep blissfully visits their eyes.
I confess, though, I'm weak, not reconciled, not so complaisant.
    What shall I do? I can't follow the precepts I preach.
Let me catch some man giving *my* dear mistress a high sign!
    Will I take it? Won't anger drive me amok?
Even when she was kissed by her very own husband, it smarted;
    I possess a love cursed with barbarous traits.
More than once this fault has injured me; *those* men are wiser,
    those who don't really mind seeing her greet other men.
Yes, it's better to shut your eyes; let her cheating be hidden
    lest she grow so bold, shame wouldn't cause her to blush.
Therefore, youths of Rome, no longer spy on your loved ones;
    let them sin and think *you've* been deceived by their guile.
People, detected, love harder; when partners are equally luckless,
    each one adds his share, causing the downfall of both.
There's a famous myth, familiar to men the world over:
    Mars and Venus were snared thanks to Vulcan, her lord.
Father Mars, inflamed by a terrible passion for Venus,
    changed from a warlike god into a prisoner of love.

Venus, than whom no goddess was ever more loving and tender,
    never was gauche; when Mars asked her, she quickly gave in.
Oh, how often (they say) she wantonly laughed at her husband's
    lameness, laughed at his hands coarsened by working with fire.
Venus gave Mars a laugh doing imitations of Vulcan;
    mixing fun with her charm, Venus was certain to please.
First they took great pains to conceal their lecherous doings;
    every single sin bore its burden of shame.
Once, though, the Sun informed on them (how can the Sun be deluded?);
    Vulcan discovered each mean trick that Venus had played.
Sun, what a bad example you set! Had you asked for her favors,
    keeping your mouth shut, *you* could have been held in her arms.
Vulcan now draped some netting over their bed and around it,
    netting so hard to detect, everyone's eyes were deceived.
Claiming he had to go to Lemnos, he let the two lovers
    meet, then down came the net: two bare lovers were caught.
Vulcan now summoned the gods to view his eminent captives;
    Venus could hardly hold back streams of tears from her eyes.
That lewd pair were unable to hide their faces, or even
    hide their private parts, covering them with their hands.
Now some jokester god called out: "Hey, Mars, if your shackles
    bother you, then why not shift them over to me?"
Neptune hotly implored to have them released, and their bodies
    set at large; Mars fled Thraceward, to Paphos went she.
What's the reward for your labors, Vulcan? Things formerly hidden
    now they openly do, no shred of shame being left.
Now you admit you were wrong, that you carried on like a madman;
    now, people say, you repent making a show of your skill.
Let such behavior be banned: that capture of Venus should tell you
    never again to set snares like the ones she endured.
Thus, you men of Rome, don't lay any traps for your rivals!
    Don't intercept their notes written in falsified hands.
Husbands, not lovers, may seize their rivals' letters and read them,
    should they think it wise—legal husbands alone!
Once again I proclaim: have fun, but keep within limits
    fixed by Roman law; leave proper ladies alone!

★

Who would dare to reveal the mystery rites of Eleusis?
   Who'd reveal the rites Samothrace jealously guards?
Keeping silence on secrets is one of the pettiest virtues;
   yet, on the other hand, blabbing is really a crime.
Good for that tattler Tantalus, snatching at out-of-reach apples,
   suffering horrible thirst plunged in the waters of Hell!
First and foremost, Venus forbids you to publish her casebooks;
   hold your tongue, or else stay away from her rites.
Though she may not hide her secrets in coffers, like Ceres,
   striking gongs of bronze wildly, to bar the profane,
still, the way her rites as performed here leads me to think that
   even here in Rome secrecy's really required.
Undraped statues of Venus show her half-stooping over;
   her discreet left hand covers her genitals up.
Animals mate in public, at all times; naturally, maidens
   shut their eyes at the sight, turning their faces away.
Well-locked bedroom doors befit *our* furtive adventures;
   out in public we hide sex organs under our robes.
Total darkness is welcome; if lacking, we mate in dense shadows;
   decent lovers find broad daylight strictly taboo.
Even of yore, when rooftiles were not yet keeping out rain or
   sunshine, when the oak furnished both shelter and food,
sex was enjoyed in a glade or in caves, not out in the open;
   even such primitive folk harbored a strong sense of shame.
Now, however, we deem our nightwork deserving of glory;
   boasting is all we've gained, bought at such a high price!
Go ahead, men, and lay all women, wherever you find them,
   just so you can tell everyone, "I had her, too!"—
just so you never lack for women to point to so proudly!
   Must each woman you touch furnish you stories of shame?
So far, minor complaints! Some men make up tales which, if true, they'd
   hotly deny: they assert every woman's been theirs.
Should her body elude them, her name is easily quoted;
   though she refused you, her good reputation is gone.
Hated guardians, keep the woman's door shut, protect her;
   place a hundred strong bolts on its obdurate posts!

What is left intact when some would-be adulterer names her,
    hoping people believe things that never took place?
As for me, even when scoring, I never relate my adventures,
    keeping my secret amours carefully hidden from all.

First and foremost, a woman's shortcomings shouldn't be faulted;
    many a woman has lied, trying to hide them away.
Perseus didn't reject Andromeda's dusky complexion,
    he whose either shoe bore a magical plume.
Everyone else found Andromache rather larger than normal;
    Hector, her husband, alone thought she was just the right size.
Things you don't like, put up with; later you'll like them; a long love
    mellows you; love that's brand-new often has finicky moods.
Till a grafted branch has grown into place and is steady,
    every breeze that blows shakes it and makes it come loose.
Soon the same tree, now that time has strengthened it, puts up resistance;
    standing strong, it will bear fruit that it didn't before.
Time, by itself, can remove each flaw and failing from bodies;
    let time pass, and faults, little by little, will go.
Many a youngster can't abide the smell of a bullhide;
    once his nose has matured, odors like that don't annoy.
Faults can be lessened by euphemisms; should she be dark-skinned,
    blacker than pitch, then say "swarthy" women are hot.
Cross-eyed? Say she's like Venus. Gray-haired? Say, like Minerva.
    Should she be dying of dire skinniness, tell her she's slim.
Should she be short, she's petite; all fat girls are pleasingly plump ones.
    Hide each minus away, cloaked by the name of a plus.

Never ask her her age or inquire what year she was born in;
    census takers are strict; *you* don't need to be, too.
This is especially wrong if her bloom is gone, and her best days
    past her, or if white hairs come to view on her comb.
Women who've reached that age are good for you, even quite old ones;
    one field will bear you grain, one field's yet to be sown.
Also, such women possess greater prudence in all of their dealings;
    they've got experience, too: *that* alone makes them adroit.

Elegant grooming makes up for the damage their years have inflicted;
   special pains that they take keep them from looking like hags.
Just as your tastes demand, they screw in a thousand positions,
   more than a painting can show, though it's inventive and clear.
Sex for them has no need of a special stimulus package;
   man and woman obtain equally all they desire.
Down with bouts in bed that leave both parties still keyed up!
   That's why sex with boys doesn't suit me at all.
Down with women who screw because they feel that they have to.
   All the while, their thoughts dwell on their knitting—too tame!
Pleasure that's looked on as duty, to me is far from a pleasure;
   who wants women to act dutiful when you're in bed?
let them utter words that openly indicate rapture,
   begging me to go slow, keeping my energy up.
Let me see my mistress wild-eyed, confessing she's conquered;
   let her grow limp and plead not to be touched for a while.
Exploits denied by Nature to raw beginners are easy
   after your strength has matured, after you've reached thirty-five.
Those in a rush, let them drink new wine; give *me* an old vintage,
   one that was stored in its jar ages and ages ago.
Only a sycamore tree that's older resists summer sunlight;
   grass that's just sprung up scratches your feet when they're bare.
Men, would you find Hermione more of a treat than her mother
   Helen, Medusa much more lovely than *her* mother was?
All who are willing to taste the charms of women who're older
   stick it out, and you'll win many a worthy reward.

Hearken! A knowing bed is burdened now by two lovers.
   Halt your flight, my Muse! Linger by locked bedroom doors!
Independent of inspiration, spontaneous chatter
   now is heard there, and now left hands come into use.
Fingers search out the places reserved for rapturous foreplay,
   places where, unobserved, Cupid's arrows are dipped.
Hector, the champion of Troy, did just the same in the old days;
   Hector wasn't just skillful in matters of war.
Great Achilles did likewise in bed with captive Briseis;

weary of fighting the foe, heroes find comfort in bed.
Yes, Briseis allowed herself to be fondled by hands which
    always were tinged with fresh blood that some Trojan had shed.
Was it that very fact that excited you, lecherous woman:
    having heroic hands eagerly feeling you up?
Trust me, the pleasures of loving shouldn't be hasty or hurried.
    No, elicit your joy slowly, take plenty of time!
After locating the spot where a lady likes to be handled,
    let no shame or false modesty shoo you away.
Look at her eyes, all asparkle with trembling flashes of lightning,
    just like the summer sun's rays reflected in pools.
Hear her moan with bliss, and hear her amorous murmurs;
    hear her uttering sighs, words that befit the event.
Don't spread too much sail and suddenly get there before her;
    yet, on the other hand, don't let her leave you behind.
Reach your goal together: *that's* when both parties are happy,
    man and maid side by side, both of them weary but glad.
Such is the course you should hold to when nothing impedes your enjoyment,
    times when no nagging fears force you to hide or to rush.
Yes, when going too slow is unsafe, add oars to your galley;
    let your horses dash, egging them on with your spur.
While your years and your strength permit it, go out and labor!
    Soon enough with its still steps old age will approach.
Either churn the sea with oars or handle the plowshare,
    maybe lend your strong hands to battles and war,
maybe use your strength and stamina servicing ladies—
    that's a type of war calling on every resource.

Book Two now is done; you grateful young men, where's my palm branch?
    Where's that myrtle wreath placed on my sweet-smelling hair?
Yes, that medic at Troy, Podalirius, proved a fine doctor;
    yes, Achilles could fight, ancient Nestor had brains;
Calchas was good at reading omens, Ajax knew weapons;
    yes, Automedon knew chariots: *I* shine in love!
Men, acclaim me your poet; men, exalt me and praise me!
    Let my name resound loudly all over the world!

Armor I've given to you like Vulcan's, bestowed on Achilles;
    just as Achilles did, *you* will prevail with that gift!
Let any man who subdues an Amazon, using my saber,
    duly inscribe on his spoils: "Ovid taught me all this."

Now the tender ladies are urging me, "Share your advice with
    us!" My dears, Book Three's wholly devoted to *you*.

BOOK THREE

Once I gave arms to the Greeks to fight the Amazons, now I'll
   lend some to Amazon queen Penthesilea as well.
Women, be equal contenders, and may those win who are favored
   both by Venus and young Cupid, who circles the globe.
Quite unfair to have unarmed women as foes to armed heroes!
   Winning that way would plunge every man into disgrace.
One fellow out of the crowd may say, "Why give a snake extra
   venom? Why entrust she-wolves with innocent sheep?"
Cease to ascribe to all women the faults of a few women only;
   let each one be judged solely by acts of her own.
True, Helen wronged Menelaus, while Agamemnon, his brother,
   died at the hands of the grim sister of Helen (what wives!);
true, Eriphyla, bribed, sent her husband off to the wars in
   Thebes, where he and his steeds, swallowed alive, went to Hell;
yet, Penelope stayed quite chaste all ten years that her husband
   fought at Troy and the ten years he was wandering lost.
Think of Laodamia, so faithful she killed herself gladly,
   following *her* man to Troy, dying before her due time.
Think of Alcestis redeeming the life of her husband Admetus,
   dying in place of him, making his funeral hers.
Didn't Evadne mount her husband's Theban pyre, calling,
   "Wait for me, Capaneus, mingle your ashes with mine!"?
Virtue's shown wearing gowns, her name is of feminine gender;
   should it be any surprise folks love that goddess so well?
Still, an art such as mine requires no lofty examples;
   I'll get along with much narrower sails on my skiff.

All of the things I teach pertain to wanton romances;
   ways that a woman is loved: such are the lessons I give.
Women don't throw flames, they don't shoot dangerous arrows;
   seldom do I observe weapons of theirs harming men.
Men are frequent deceivers; tender women, much less so.
   Just inquire, and you'll find very few blamed for that crime.
Jason deserted Medea, who'd borne him children already;
   then he clutched a new bride close to his treacherous breast.
Theseus made Ariadne afraid of the beachcombing seagulls,
   leaving her high and dry there on an isle all unknown.
Ask why a single road is called *Nine* Roads: there lonely Phyllis
   gazed nine times out to sea; mourning her, trees shed their leaves.
Even pious Aeneas, a guest of Dido's in Carthage,
   planted a sword in her heart, making her take her own life.
All those women were doomed through lack of amorous knowhow;
   all of them needed my art; art eternizes love.
Women would still be unknowing, but Venus bade me instruct them;
   right before my eyes goddess Venus appeared!
"Why do the wretched ladies deserve such trouble," she asked me,
   "all that defenseless crowd subject to men who bear arms?
Your Books One and Two have made men skillful exploiters;
   women have to be taught love by your lessons, as well.
That Greek poet Stesichorus badmouthed Helen; recanting,
   singing her praises, he gained greater results with his lyre.
Ovid, I know you well (don't injure women of culture!),
   all your livelong days *you* must depend on their grace."
Falling silent, she then from the myrtle encircling her tresses
   handed me one leaf, several berries as well;
taking them, I could sense the heavenly force that was in them;
   purer shone the sky; how lighthearted I felt!
While she is still inspiring me, come and learn from me, ladies
   (those who're less strict, but obey modesty, law, and the right)!
Even now bear in mind that old age surely is coming;
   don't let an hour pass by wasted that might be well spent.
While you may, while the springtime of life still sweetly adorns you,
   have your fun; years go by just like a hastening brook.
Waters already gone past can never be made to flow upstream;

time that's flown won't come back to you ever again.
Make good use of your youth, for time speeds by with a swift foot,
    never restoring the heights once achieved in your prime.
There where I now see barren plots, once violets blossomed;
    roses for garlands adorned bushes where now I see thorns.
Days will come when women who now shut their doors on their lovers
    find themselves sleeping alone, old and cold in the night.
Then their doors won't be smashed in a nighttime fight, and their thresholds
    won't be strewn with red roses when morning returns.
Oh, how quickly, I fear, are bodies disfigured by wrinkles!
    My, but color can fade fast from a beautiful face!
Some may claim to have had a few gray hairs even in girlhood;
    now that gray will spread quickly all over their head.
Snakes, it is said, slough off their years when they slough off their old skins;
    stags that lose their horns aren't turned old by that loss.
Human happiness flees when unaided: gather the blossoms;
    blossoms ungathered soon fall as they wither away.
Furthermore, days of youth are shortened by every confinement;
    fields that are constantly reaped soon get exhausted and fail.
Moon, your love for handsome Endymion wasn't disgraceful;
    Cephalus, loved by Dawn, caused that goddess no shame.
Venus, with only mourned Adonis to love, would have never
    borne Aeneas of Troy, mothered Cadmus's bride.
Emulate, mortal women, those deities' shining examples;
    don't rob lustily hot men of your lovable charms.
What will you lose if they fool you? You still will have tested those pleasures.
    Taste them a thousand times: pleasures like those aren't lost.
Iron will wear away, and flints lose substance from handling;
    private parts live on, never afraid they'll get worn.
Who forbids you to light your torch from another that's offered?
    Who would refuse you a drink, owning a bottomless well?
Thus, when a woman complains, "This isn't the time or the place, sir,"
    isn't the water you seek wasted unless it is drawn?
These instructions won't make you wanton; they'll keep you from fearing
    ills that are fanciful. Give! Don't be afraid of a loss!
Soon I'll be carried away on the wings of a wind that's much stronger;
    now, while I'm still in port, let a mild breeze waft me forth.

★

Grooming's my first concern: doesn't Bacchus foster well-tended
    grapevines? Doesn't the wheat thrive in a field free of weeds?
Beauty's a gift from the gods, and not many women can claim it.
    Most of you never obtain gifts so great and so rare.
Forms, looked after, will prosper. Neglect them, you'll surely regret it,
    even when they're at first lovely as Venus's form.
True, the women of old were not such sticklers for grooming:
    that's because their men used to be rough and raw, too.
Yes, Andromache's tunics were virtually made out of sacking.
    What's so strange about that? Soldier husbands were tough.
Had you been married to Ajax, would *you* have approached him all dolled up,
    seeing his armor of hides (seven oxhides, to wit)?
Ages ago, life was simple and plain, but Rome now is golden;
    now it possesses wealth garnered all over the world.
Look at the Capitol hill of today and compare it with old days:
    you'd say different Joves lived on it back then and now.
Look at our Senate house, now worthy of such an assembly;
    back in Sabine times, thatch composed it, and straw.
Now the Palatine gleams with the homes of our Prince and Apollo;
    way back then it was just pasture where oxen would graze.
Others may dote on the past: I'm grateful I wasn't alive till
    now: our current ways suit me right down to the ground.
Not because refractory gold is dug from the earth now;
    not because rare shells reach us from faraway shores;
not because our hills are dwindling, plundered for marble;
    not because sea walls put blue waters to flight;
no, it's because it's an age of refinement we live in; no rustic
    manners remain such as flawed Grandfather's primitive days.

Ladies, refrain from weighing your ears down with gems and the pearls which
    dark-skinned Indians cull, diving in waters of green.
Don't clump around with the weight of the gold sewn into your garments;
    riches you hope will allure often chase us away.
Cleanliness, neatness attract us; don't let your hair be disheveled;
    hands that are deftly applied add to your charms or subtract.
Nor is there only one form of adorning yourselves: pick the fittest,
    pick what's suited to you. Mirrors will help you to judge.

Should your face be long, fix your hair with an unadorned parting;
    Laodamia fixed hers *that* way, and no other way.
Rounded faces require that a very small knot of the hair be
    tied at the top of the head, leaving the two ears exposed.
One woman lets her hair hang all the way down to her shoulders;
    that's how Apollo wears his, singing low to the lyre.
Other women can bind their hair back like huntress Diana
    out on a spirited chase, hitching her skirts with a belt.
Some women look their best when their hair is billowing loosely;
    others, when their hair's tightly confined by a band.
Some need adornments of tortoiseshell (once Mercury carved it
    into Apollo's lyre); some, robes folded in waves.
Just as the acorns on wide-branching ilexes cannot be counted,
    nor Mount Hybla's bees, nor the beasts in the Alps,
I can't count all the methods that women use to look lovely;
    every passing day adds to the staggering sum.
Sometimes a feigned neglect of her hair is appealing. You'd think her
    hair wasn't combed for a day, yet it was minutes ago.
Art may imitate chance: when Iole's city had fallen,
    Hercules, love-stricken, said: "This is the maiden for me!"
That's how you looked, Ariadne (deserted on Naxos), when Bacchus
    lifted you onto his car (satyrs were shouting with joy).
Ladies, how kindly your beauty is treated by Nature! Your defects
    all can be mended and cured *so* many wonderful ways!
Men are often left bald, or with hairlines swiftly receding,
    just as when cold north winds fiercely detach every leaf.
Women can dye their gray hair with marvelous German decoctions;
    thanks to their skill, they look better than natural blondes.
Women walk out in the street with thick, thick hair that's been purchased;
    money's the magic charm changing the old into new.
Nor is it shameful to buy hair; we see it publicly vended
    right in front of the shrine Muses and Hercules share.
What shall I say of your clothes, ladies? Can't you see I've no use for
    appliqués, nor for wools purpled by Tyrian dyes?
Finding available less expensive coloring matters,
    why so insanely wear all of your cash on your back?
Can't you wear clear blue shades, the color of skies that are cloudless,

not turned gray by rain brought by southerly winds?
Can't you wear golden hues, like the ram on which Phrixus and Helle
    fled from Ino, a mean mother-in-law, as they flew?
One color imitates water, and thus is referred to as "glaucous";
    yes, I believe the nymphs usually dressed in that hue.
One color imitates saffron; dewy Aurora wears saffron
    driving her mettlesome steeds, bringing the light of the dawn.
This hue is like green myrtles from Paphos, and that hue resembles
    amethysts. *This* is like white roses; and that, like gray cranes.
This hue is brown as shepherd girls' acorns; that one's like almonds;
    wax's yellow hue graces many a fleece.
So many flowers appear when the earth is refreshed in the springtime,
    vines are producing buds, winter's doldrums are gone!
That's how many colors wool can absorb. When you choose them,
    choose them well; not all colors become each of you.
Dark ones are good if you're pale-skinned: dark ones suited Briseis;
    captured by Greeks, she wore dark gray garments at Troy.
Light ones are good if you're dark: Andromeda, white-clad, was gorgeous;
    envy made the gods torment Seriphos, her isle.

Oh, how close I came to warning you: no smelly armpits;
    no coarse hair on your legs, ugly and rough to the touch!
Then I recalled I was not addressing Near Eastern hill tribes,
    women who drink from the streams Asia Minor contains.
Why do I need to teach you to care for your teeth, lest they darken,
    teach you to wash your face thoroughly when you wake up?
Surely you know how to whiten your skin with layers of powder.
    Cheeks not a natural red? Rectify that with some rouge!
Skillfully use every means to blacken the bareness of eyebrows;
    beauty patches adorn cheeks that, without them, are plain.
Don't be afraid to enhance the allure of your eyes with cold ashes;
    also use saffron, which grows close to streams in the East.
I wrote a very short book on cosmetics for feminine faces
    (short, but I took great pains doing the research involved).
Read it, it offers protection from defects that threaten your beauty.
    Your concerns are mine; *my* skill is at your command.
Yet, don't leave the containers spread out on tables: your lover's

liable to find them. Hide artifice, so it can work.
Lovers will be put off by the junk you smear on your faces,
    crud so heavy it slips, landing inside of your dress.
Lanolin ointment stinks, though it may be imported from Athens,
    taken from filthy fleece, sheep sweat, dirt, and the like.
Never be seen by others taking a doe-marrow mixture,
    openly scouring your teeth, letting everyone watch.
Yes, it will add to your charms, but it's really ghastly to look at.
    Yet, things ugly when half-finished may please you when done.
Statues that now are treasures because they were sculptured by Myron
    once were blocks of stone, hard and crude and inert.
Gold will have to be crushed before it makes rings for your fingers;
    clothes you delight to wear once were contemptible wool.
During their fashioning, fabulous gems were just mineral fragments;
    now they show Venus nude, wringing her sea-spattered hair.
Thus, while you make up your face, let's imagine you're off somewhere sleeping;
    don't let us see you until every last dab is applied.
Why do I need to know the cause of your face's pure whiteness?
    Shut the door to your room! No rough sketches for me!
Men aren't meant to be shown your secrets, most of which surely
    give them pain when they're not carefully hidden away.
Theaters are all decorated with statues splendid and golden;
    study them closely, they're just wood that's covered with foil.
People aren't allowed to approach them till they are finished.
    Thus, don't primp and paint while there's a man looking on.
Still, I don't forbid your combing your hair in his presence,
    so that it freely flows down your back in a stream.
Men around? Then I admonish you: never be cross or be sullen.
    Don't keep loosening combed hair, or allow it to fall.
Don't attack your maid while she dresses you; don't let me hear you've
    scratched her face with your nails, jabbed her arm with a pin.
Battered servants curse their mistress's head when they comb it;
    bleeding, they weep hot tears, handling the hair that they hate.
Should your hair be too thin, have the door to your room closely guarded,
    dress where no men are allowed (use the Good Goddess's shrine).
Once a woman I knew was informed of my sudden arrival;
    flustered, she put on her wig, getting it wrong way around.

Only on foes would I wish such embarrassing, deadly disasters;
    let such disgraces befall Parthian women, say I!
Cattle with broken horns are hideous, so is a grassless
    field or a tree without leaves; hairless heads are the worst.

Semele, Leda (Jove's loves), you have no need of my lessons;
    nor does Europa, who crossed seas on a make-believe bull;
nor does Helen, whom Menelaus (not foolishly) called for,
    while, no fool himself, Paris retained her in Troy.
Ordinary women, both homely and beautiful, want my
    services, and the plain always outnumber the fair.
Those who are lovely can have no need of my art or my precepts;
    they have a dowry, plus beauty that calls for no art.
Sailors, when seas are calm, relax and go about carefree;
    yet, when the seas run high, sailors pray for some aid.
Only very seldom are faces faultless, so hide those
    faults; every way you can, hide each bodily flaw.
Short women ought to sit, so they don't seem to sit when they're standing;
    they're so tiny, they'd best lie on their couches all day.
Even then, to avoid being measured and gauged as they lie there,
    shorties should have a spread robe concealing their feet.
Women too skinny should wear only wide, voluminous garments;
    loosely let them hang down from your shoulders, my dears.
Pallid ladies should add to their color with striping of purple;
    dark ones ought to put on linen from Egypt (it's white!).
Feet misshapen, conceal in sandals of snowy-white leather;
    fleshless ankles should stay always firmly encased.
Scapulas rising too high call for shoulder pads (but discreet ones);
    should your chest be too flat, wind some sashes around.
Women with pudgy fingers or ugly fingernails ought to
    make only very slight gestures whenever they speak.
Those with malodorous breath should always eat before talking;
    let them stand at a fair distance from those that they love.
Should you have a tooth that is black or enormous or crooked,
    take care not to laugh; laughter can often bring tears.

★

Unbelievable! Still, I have to teach women to laugh right!
    Even that natural act has to be modestly done.
Mouths shouldn't open too wide or display a huge pair of dimples;
    let the rims of your lips hide the tops of your teeth.
Never let your sides be heaving with laughter that's endless;
    let your laughs be light, soft in a feminine way.
Never let your face be distorted by ghastly guffawing;
    some women laugh so hard, people would think that they wept.
One woman's much too shrill, her laughter is far from appealing;
    she-donkeys turning a mill bray exactly like that.
Yes, my art has few limits! I teach the decorum of weeping,
    when and where to cry, how to carry it off.
What if a woman's words are not pronounced as they should be?
    What if a girlish lisp's always obstructing her tongue?
Some ladies find this fault so charming they do it on purpose,
    training themselves to speak worse than expected of them.
Pay attention to all these matters; they'll aid and assist you.
    Learn how to walk with grace, taking ladylike steps.
Walking involves an amount of tact that's not to be sneezed at,
    luring or driving away men you haven't yet met.
This woman sways to and fro most artfully, catching the breeze in
    flowing folds of her gown, haughtily stepping along;
that woman walks like the wife of some redneck up in the mountains,
    taking enormous strides, shambling with legs far apart.
Many things want moderation, and so does this; for one gait was
    rustic, the other was too mincing to tickle our taste.
Still, let the lower part of your shoulder be bare, and the upper
    part of your arm, as well, readily viewed from your left.
This suits women who're fair-skinned; whenever I see them bare-shouldered,
    I'm compelled to kiss women right on that spot.

Sweetly singing, the Sirens, those ancient maritime marvels,
    stopped every ship passing by, swiftly though it might sail.
Hearing them, sly Ulysses, tied to the mast, nearly broke loose
    (all the rest of the crew stuffed their ears up with wax).
Song is a winning ploy; let every woman learn singing;
    many get men in their beds that way, instead of by looks.

Let them reprise the songs they're heard in marble-clad theaters,
    times that mimes have sung, acting like men of the Nile.
Let no lady pupil of mine be unable to hold a
    plectrum firm in her right hand, a guitar in her left.
Thracian Orpheus charmed wild beasts with his lyre and made rocks move,
    stirring the lakes of Hell, soothing its three-headed dog.
Also, the song of Amphion, his mother's avenger, had such might,
    stones of their own accord formed the ramparts of Thebes.
Though a dolphin is mute, it isn't deaf: in the legend
    one, responsive to song, carried Arion to shore.
Ladies, also practice that party-time harp from Phoenicia,
    strumming with right hand and left; harps enliven a feast.

Learn the verse of Callimachus, learn the verse of Philitas;
    learn the verse of that old drunkard Anacreon, too.
Memorize Sappho's poems (who ever was lewder than she was?);
    study Menander's plays (masters deluded by slaves).
Be prepared to read the works of the tender Propertius,
    Gallus's poems of love, yes—Tibullus's, too!
Read the story of Phrixus and Helle, related by Varro,
    how that golden fleece caused her to drown in the strait.
Read of Aeneas the refugee, ancient sire of our nation:
    Vergil's epic's the best ever yet published in Rome.
One day, perhaps, my name will be mentioned along with those great ones;
    maybe my writings will last, saved from oblivion, too.
Maybe someone will say: "Read the elegant works of our poet;
    those three scrolls contain wisdom for women and men.
Either select from his *Loves* some passage and softly recite it,
    chanting with flexible voice, charming each listener there;
otherwise, take up his book called *Heroines' Letters* and read it.
    He invented that work; no one had done it before."
May that come true, Apollo! You fostering spirits of old bards,
    Bacchus (god with horns), Muses: make it come true!

Who could doubt that I also require my pupils to dance well,
    gracefully weaving their arms after the wine has been poured?
All applaud professional dancers seen in a theater

wagging their sides; they please all with their movements so free.
Maybe it's paltry advice, but a woman should also play dice well,
    knowing what every throw signifies during the game.
Now let her cast three dice, and now let her stop and consider
    which is the side she should join, which one to challenge or "call."
Let her be cautious, let her be shrewd when she plays Little Robbers;
    one of her pieces, when two others attack it, may fall.
Warrior pieces bereft of their partners will have to keep battling;
    their opponents may still need to return as they came.
Other times, let smooth balls be randomly placed in an open
    net, where you must take out one without moving the rest.
One game, astutely devised, makes use of lines on a gameboard,
    twelve, like the months in a year silently slipping away.
Either side of that little board has three pieces to play with;
    get them all in a row, then that game has been won.
Many such games can be invented; a woman who can't play
    loses face, for love often is won in a game.
Making intelligent throws, though, may be the least of your problems:
    keeping a level head's more important by far.
Gambling, we lose our caution, exposing our inner emotions;
    overexcited, we let thoughts be revealed as we play.
Anger arises (an ugly feeling) and greediness, also;
    quarrels break out, and fights, grief that gnaws at our heart.
Insults are flung about and the air is blue with our curses;
    everyone wrathfully calls gods to speed to their aid.
One player, losing his all, wants his slate wiped clean; and I've often
    seen the bitter tears coursing down many a cheek.
May great Jupiter free you from such disgusting behavior,
    women whose aim is to win men by your grace and your charm!

Women can play these games of a far from strenuous nature;
    men, on the other hand, find there are more they can choose.
Men can play with swift balls, with javelins, hoops, or with weapons;
    men can ride a horse trotting in circles, as well.
Women don't train on the Field of Mars or cool off in the Virgin's
    waters; nor do they swim Tiber's peaceable stream.
Yes, you can stroll under Pompey's Portico, taking the shade there

during August, when steeds driven by Virgo bring heat.
Visit the Palatine hill with its temple of bay-crowned Apollo
    (*that* god sank the ships Cleopatra equipped).
Visit the monuments honoring sister and wife of Augustus,
    trophies his son-in-law won (mighty Agrippa) at sea.
Look at the altars that burn with incense for Isis the heifer;
    visit our theaters three, taking conspicuous seats.
See the arena, whose sand is always flecked with fresh bloodstains;
    see the turning-post racing chariots pass.
Things concealed aren't known, and things unknown aren't sought for:
    faces unlooked upon can't lead to a pleasant result.
Even musicians as great as Thamyras, great as Amoebeus,
    should they remain unknown, never get credit for skill.
Had the famed Apelles never done paintings of Venus,
    Venus would still be immersed down in the depths of the sea.
What do the hallowed bards all seek, if not reputation?
    All our labors you'll find centered on wishes for fame.
Once we poets were dear to the gods, and kings entertained us;
    choirs at civic events won outstanding awards.
Poets were sanctified then, their names revered and respected;
    often appreciable wealth fell to their lot as a prize.
Ennius, though he was born in remote Calabrian mountains,
    earned a place at great General Scipio's side.
Now poets' ivy is honorless; vigils devoted to learning,
    love for the Muse, people call laziness: such are the times!
Yet, it brings profit to yearn for fame: who'd know about Homer,
    had his *Iliad* lain hidden, which now is acclaimed?
Who would know about Jove's love Danae, had she been always
    locked in her tower until age had withered her looks?
Crowds are of use to you, lovely ladies; let your feet often
    stray past your own front door; gladly mingle with throngs.
Where the sheep are numerous, she-wolves can pick out a fine one;
    Jupiter's eagle swoops down on birds in a flock.
Therefore, let the people have leave to see beautiful women;
    out of that number, perhaps one will be drawn to their charms.
Women desirous of pleasing men should be seen in all places,
    paying strictest heed always to looking their best.
Everywhere chance plays a part; let your hook be constantly dangling;

just when you think it's no go, lo! you've caught you a fish!
Frequently hunting hounds roam all in vain through the forest,
    while an undriven stag blunders into your net.
Tied to her rock, Andromeda hardly could hope that some hero,
    moved by her tears, would arrive, slaying monsters for her.
Often new husbands are found at old husbands' funerals; looking
    sad with your hair let down, bawling away, never hurts.

Yet, shun men who take too much pride in their looks and appearance,
    deftly arranging their hair, keeping it neatly in place.
Yes, they'll spin you a yarn, but they've told it to thousands of women;
    love like theirs will stray, free from ties that could last.
What is a lady to do when her lover is slicker than *she* is?
    Maybe he has more men firing his fancy than she!
Take it from me, though it's hard to believe: Troy'd never have fallen,
    had it forestalled the doom seeress Cassandra announced.
Some men plan their attack by falsely pretending they love you,
    seeking a shameful gain via a ploy such as that.
Don't be fooled by their hair, all shiny with sweet-smelling lotions,
    nor by the tongue of their tight belt that wrinkles their robes.
Don't let their toga deceive you, however finely it's woven;
    don't be beguiled if they wear numerous rings on their hands.
Maybe the one who's most dapper among them will finally rob you;
    maybe he's wanted your rich dress, not you, all along.
"Give it back!" is the frequent cry of victimized women,
    "Give it back!" And the whole Forum resounds with their voice.
Venus watches those brawls from her nearby glittering temple,
    calmly, along with the nymphs lodged in the Appian fount.
Though there's no doubt of the bad reputation earned by some heroes,
    many more men than you think jilt their sweethearts each day.
Learn from the woes of other women to fear for your own woes;
    never leave your door open to men who deceive.
Maids of Athens, don't trust any promise sworn to by Theseus:
    true, he may call on the gods; yet, he has done so before.
And Demophoon, too, his son and the heir to his cheating,
    toyed with Phyllis and left no good name in his wake.
Should men promise a lot, return an equivalent promise;

should they give you gifts, render contractual joys.
Women receiving gifts and then refusing requital
    might even quench the flame Vestal Virgins protect,
might even steal the holy objects stored in a temple,
    might even give their men hemlock and poison to drink!

Now I must center in on my subject. Muse, pull the reins in!
    Hasten no longer on wheels wildly rotating, my Muse.
Let a love note on tablets of fir arrange for a meeting;
    let a trusted maid carry his letter to you.
Study it; from the words he's written there, make a decision
    whether he's telling a lie, whether his pain is sincere.
After a short while, answer him; often a lover kept waiting
    burns more fiercely—but don't keep him waiting too long!
Never make your defeat too easy for love-hungry suitors,
    nor deny their request harshly, either: keep calm!
Make him hope and despair at the same time; see that your answers
    give him more and more hope, less despair every time.
Ladies, let your letters be well expressed, but in normal,
    everyday language; write plainly, for that's what men like.
Oh, how often a letter has pained an insecure lover!
    Oh, how extravagant words nullify beautiful looks!
Yes, though you may not wear the headbands of housewives and matrons,
    still it's your job to deceive men who are lords of your life;
therefore, have your letters written by slaves or by handmaids;
    send no tokens to youths unfamiliar to you.
Men who keep such tokens deserve your contempt, but the tokens
    carry the force of Jove's thunderbolts, nevertheless.
Women who might be blackmailed are usually pallid with terror,
    living for ever so long under somebody's thumb.
Fraud, in my opinion, may justly be countered by *more* fraud;
    laws allow you to wield weapons when foemen are armed.
Train your *one* hand to write in numerous hands, for your safety.
    (May those men who incite counsels like this go to Hell!)
Don't make replies on a tablet he's sent till you've leveled the surface,
    lest the wax reveal traces of *your* hand and his.

Let the lover you write to be always addressed as a woman;
　　let your note read "she," though the recipient's "he."

Please permit me now to turn from small things to big things;
　　let me crowd on sail, borne by a favoring wind.
Part of being lovely is checking impetuous mood swings;
　　wrath is all right for beasts, men want the blessings of peace.
Anger swells up your face; your veins fill with blood and they blacken;
　　eyes will glint with ire fierce as Medusa's, or worse.
"Off with you, flute, you're not worth the risk of looking so puffy!"
　　Pallas Athena cried, seeing her face in a stream.
You, too, ladies, will cease to rage if you look in a mirror;
　　there you'll find your face unrecognizably warped.
No less hurtful to beauty is pridefulness, faces too haughty;
　　love must be lured by eyes charmingly gentle and sweet.
Yes, immoderate pride is hateful (trust in an expert);
　　yes, all too often men hate an imperious gaze.
Look at those looking at *you;* if they smile, smile back and be pleasant;
　　should a polite man nod, show him you've seen it, and nod.
Cupid will drop wooden swords on witnessing similar preludes;
　　then he'll pull out the sharp darts from his quiver and shoot.
Sorrowful women are pains; though Ajax loved captive Tecmessa,
　　Romans are out for a laugh; cheerful ladies for us!
No, Andromache! No, Tecmessa! I'd never have wanted
　　either of you two bleak women as mistress of mine.
Yes, your children *make* me believe, but it's hard to believe that
　　two crybabies like you ever slept with your men.
Am I really to think that his gloomy woman called Ajax
　　"light of my life" or spoke words likely to give a man joy?

Who says lofty things can't be used as examples for small things?
　　Who says I can't respect famous generals' names?
Skillful generals place one man in charge of a hundred;
　　one man's the cavalry chief; one guards the banners of war.
You, too, ladies: decide on your lovers' proper employment;
　　study their ways, then give each one the place he deserves.

Rich ones ought to make presents; a legist should aid with his counsel;
    lawyers with eloquent ways ought to defend you in court.
We, the bards, should be asked to send you nothing but poems;
    more than anyone else, poets are suited for love.
No one's a better herald of beauty than we are when smitten:
    famed is Tibullus's dear lady; Propertius's, too.
Known in the East and the West in "Lycoris," mistress of Gallus;
    many ask *me:* "In your *Loves,* who's that 'Corinna' you praise?"
Furthermore, poets are sacred and shun all treacherous dealings;
    arts that we all profess cause our ways to improve.
Worldly ambition is not for us, nor avarice, either;
    business leaves us cold; give us a couch in the shade!
Yet, we're readily hooked, and we burn with powerful passion;
    poets' love is a love certainly going to last.
Surely, the placid craft we practice softens our natures;
    all our actions befit poetry's peaceable art.
Ladies, be good to us poets who emulate those of Boeotia;
    bards have a godlike force; Muses smile on their work.
Deity dwells in poets, they carry on commerce with heaven;
    poets' spirits have come down from abodes in the sky.
Hoping for gifts from learned bards is a criminal notion.
    Woe is me, it's a crime none of the ladies avoid!
Yet, good women, conceal your greed, and don't let your faces
    show it too clearly; new lovers will flee from the snare.
Horsemen won't use the selfsame bit on steeds that have just now
    first experienced reins tugging, and steeds that are trained.
Nor should you ladies follow the selfsame pathway to capture
    both a man of mature years and an innocent boy.
That young fellow, still green and new to the warfare of Cupid,
    comes to your bedroom door just like new booty you've won.
Let him know you alone, be his one and only attachment;
    strong, high fences must guard grainfields as tender as that.
See that you have no rivals; if you alone please him, you'll hold him.
    Neither love nor kings' rule can submit to be shared.
That mature man, though, will love you less soon, but more wisely;
    he'll put up with a lot raw recruits wouldn't take.
He won't break down your doors or burn them with jealous emotions;

he won't resort to his nails, fiercely clawing your cheeks.
He won't rip his mistress's robes or tear his own tunic;
   he won't pull your hair, loosing a deluge of tears.
Doings like those befit a young, excitable lover;
   that maturer man suffers with stoical calm.
He will burn like damp hay, with a slow and smothered combustion,
   just like fresh-cut logs hauled from a forested ridge.
Love like his is firmer; the younger man's, fertile but briefer.
   Seize the fruit with a swift hand as it hurries away!

Let all secrets be known, once you've opened your gates to the foeman;
   let's earn trustful faith, even when treason's at work.
Favors readily granted won't foster a love that's enduring;
   sometimes, not often, give up cheerfulness, standing aloof.
Let the man sprawl outside your front door, crying, "How cruel!"
   Let him now implore, now make many a threat.
Sweetness is hard on a man, we find bitter potions refreshing;
   often a favoring wind sinks the skiff it should aid.
Why do men have such trouble adoring legitimate spouses?—
   men can take them to bed any old time that they like.
Put a door in their way, let a doorkeeper say to those husbands
   harshly, "No, you can't!"—love will come, once they're shut out.
Off now with blunted foils, it's time for swords that are sharpened;
   I've no doubt that my own weapons will turn against *me*.
While your newfound lover is caught in your net and still thrashing,
   let him hope he alone owns all the rights to your charms.
Only later allow him to sense that he shares with a rival
   bed and charms alike; otherwise, watch him grow cold.
Bravehearted horses race best when, released from the starting gate's confines,
   they can see foes to pursue, horses they need to outrun.
Flames of love, though flickering out, flare up when the lover's
   hurt; as for me, I confess, only my hurts make me love.
Yet, don't let the cause of his pain be too easily noted;
   let him, sunken in grief, guess much more than he knows.
Seeing you well protected by so-called slaves will inflame him;
   so will a too severe husband's vigilant eye.
Pleasure that falls in our laps too safely won't find us receptive;

though you're as bold as a whore, make him believe you're afraid.
Even when no one's guarding your door, let him in through a window;
    make your features express fear that you don't really feel.
Let some crafty maid barge in on you, crying, "We're done for!"
    Hide the trembling lad any place wits can devise.
Yet, a palpable love must accompany all of those terrors;
    otherwise he won't think nights with you are worthwhile.

Damn it! I nearly omitted the ways of deluding a clever
    husband, or maybe a shrewd guard with eyes in his head.
Wives should fear their spouses, it's right that wives should be guarded;
    that's proper, that's what the law, modesty, justice demand.
Yet, you former slave girls, recently granted your freedom,
    scruples aren't for you. Learn from me how to deceive!
Let as many keep watch as Argus had eyes (yes, a hundred!);
    make up your mind to deceive all those guards, and you will!
Say, is one of them spying to see that you don't write a love note
    while you're supposed to employ times like those for a bath?
Tell me, what good is that guard, when your maid can carry a letter
    hidden beneath her robe, fastened with wide strips of cloth?
When she can hide a missive that's firmly tied to her shinbone?
    When her sandal conceals passionate words you have sent?
Should your watchers catch on to *that* method, then have your handmaid
    offer her back to your pen, bearing your words on her skin.
Letters written in fresh milk safely elude the observer;
    sprinkle on charcoal dust, then they're easily read.
Use a stalk of moist flax to write an untraceable letter;
    let the tablet's plain wood hide your message from all.
Argive King Acrisius, Danae's father, was watchful;
    yet, he, too, was called Grandfather, thanks to her sin.
What is a guard to do when the city has so many theaters,
    racetracks where women enjoy seeing the horses in teams,
temples for shaking their rattles in honor of Isis of Egypt,
    places to go to where male guardians aren't allowed?
(See: the Good Goddess forbids the presence of males in her temple,
    save for those whom the sly women expressly invite!)
Don't the public baths afford women places to frisk in

83

while their attendant men guard their clothing outside?
Also, each time it pays off, a girlfriend can "fall ill" and share your
   bed and, "sick" as she is, yield up her place to a man.
Also, as false as its name, a key can teach you deception,
   so it's not your front door, only, that lets people in.
Also, a watchman will doze when plenty of wine is supplied him,
   even inferior wine grown on a hillside in Spain.
Furthermore, there are drugs that induce a long-lasting slumber;
   eyes made drowsy by drugs sleep in oblivious peace.
Loyal servant girls can hold a hated observer
   lovingly by their side, feigning, detaining him there.
Why beat around the bush, why parcel out paltry instructions,
   when even minimal bribes buy a guardian off?
Bribery, trust me, works on humans and works on the gods, too;
   Jupiter, offered gifts, also is readily bought.
What are the wise to do when fools delight in a present?
   Wise men will also accept gifts and stay mute as a fish.
Guardians, though, must be bought securely, for now and the future;
   then they'll always renew favors they've done you before.
Earlier on, I recall, I said, "Place no trust in companions";
   that lament concerned men, but you, too, are involved.
Be too trusting, ladies, and others will seize on your lovers;
   hares that you've caught, you'll find hunted all over again.
Women who share their beds and rooms with me, though not my mistress,
   often, believe me, receive regular visits from me.
Therefore, don't let the maid who waits on you be too attractive;
   often she'll play the part mistresses, only, should play.

Madman, you're carried away! Why attack the foe without armor?
   Why do I drop my guard, letting such evidence leak?
Birds don't tell the fowlers where and when to locate them;
   deer don't teach the hounds, hostile to them, how to run.
Who cares whether it profits me? Loyally on with my lessons!
   Murderous Lemian wives, kill me with swords I've supplied!
Ladies, make us believe you love us (really, it's easy);
   men who are eager enough readily offer their trust.
Let a woman just gaze on a youth more lovingly; let her
   sigh deep sighs and ask why he's arriving so late.

Let her add a few tears and pretend he has given her rivals;
    let her claw that youth's cheeks with redoubtable nails.
Then he's already convinced; he'll offer sympathy gladly,
    telling himself, "This poor woman's upset over *me!*"
Should he, especially, be a fashion plate, pleased with his mirror,
    he'll imagine he's got goddesses falling for him.
Yet, however much he irks you, inhibit your anger;
    hearing of rivals, do not lose your wits all at once.
Don't be too quick to believe, though; Procris, suspecting her husband
    wrongly, got herself killed. Risky, such hasty belief!

Close to the shining, blossoming slopes of Hymettus, near Athens,
    spurts a sacred spring; green grass softens the ground.
Low trees stand in a grove, with arbutus shrubs in abundance.
    Rosemary, myrtle, and bay fill the air with their scent.
Dense-leaved box trees are there, and tamarisks easily broken;
    tender laburnums you'll find, also elegant pines.
Plants of all these kinds, and the tips of the grass, were atremble,
    fanned by a breeze from the west, cooled by salubrious winds.
Cephalus peacefully slept. He'd left his hounds and his beaters;
    this was a nook that the youth often chose for a nap.
"Wandering Breeze," he sang, "today I'm feeling too warm, so
    come relieve me, come cool this hot bosom of mine!"
Someone, far too attentive, repeated the words he had heard there
    faithfully into the shy ears of the young hunter's wife.
Procris, hearing the name of Breeze and fearing a rival,
    fainted; her terrible grief left her suddenly mute.
Pale she turned as the leaves on a vine whose grapes have been gathered,
    leaves that winter's grim onset has drained of their green;
pale as the ripened quinces that bend the boughs, they're so heavy;
    pale as dogberries not fit yet for humans to eat.
Coming to, she ripped her thin, light robe from her bosom,
    wounding her guiltless cheeks wildly with merciless nails.
Then she raced through the streets, her tresses streaming behind her,
    frenzied as Maenads become, prodded by Bacchus's staff.
Nearing her husband's nook, she left her friends in the valley;
    bravely she entered the grove, tiptoeing secretly in.

What was her state of mind as she lurked there insanely and waited?
　　What fire burned in her sad heart, all maddened with grief?
Surely she thought that that Breeze, whoever she was, would be coming;
　　surely she thought her moist eyes would witness a crime.
Now she was sorry she came, for she didn't want to expose him,
　　now she was glad; thus, love made her wishes confused.
There to inspire belief were the place and the name and the tattler;
　　also, excited minds think their fears must be real.
Noting the mark on the grass of a form that had clearly reclined there,
　　Procris felt her heart pounding away in her breast.
Now full noon had arrived and had shortened the tenuous shadows,
　　sunset and break of day each at an equal remove.
Cephalus, Mercury's son, had now returned to the forest,
　　dashing onto his cheeks cooling drops from the spring.
Procris still hid, in distress; her husband lay down on his grass plot,
　　saying, "Come now, you soft west winds; come now, you breeze!"
Now her amusing mistake was explained to the listening Procris;
　　now she regained her calm; color returned to her face.
Rising in hopes she would soon be clasped in her husband's embraces,
　　Procris made the leaves rustle, speeding along.
Cephalus, thinking some quarry was there, with juvenile fervor
　　stirred his limbs; in his right hand his weapon he held.
Luckless man, what are you doing? It's no beast, away with your weapon!
　　Woe is me! Your wife's pierced by the arrow you shot.
Procris exclaimed: "Ah, me! You've struck a heart that was friendly,
　　one that has always borne wounds inflicted by you.
Dying before my time, still I wasn't insulted by rivals!
　　Earth, this will make you lie lightly over my corpse.
Now I exhale my breath into breezes I wrongly suspected.
　　Now I'm slipping away; close my eyes, cherished hand!"
Cephalus held his lady's body against his pained bosom,
　　Procris's cruel wound washed by tears from his eyes.
Then her spirit departed and, slowly deserting imprudent
　　Procris, was caught on the sad lips of the miserable man.

Now I return to my task; I now have to touch on some bare facts,
　　hoping my weary ship's finally entering port.

Nervously, ladies, you've waited to hear my instructions on dinner
    parties; now take my arm, let me usher you in.
Make a late entrance, befitting your status, after the lamps are
    lit; coming late is a plus, lateness is best of all bawds.
Homely though you may be, you'll look attractive to tosspots;
    darkness of night will veil every one of your flaws.
Pick up the food with your fingers; win points by your manner of eating;
    don't let soiled hands rub grease all over your face.
Don't eat a snack before coming from home; leave room in your stomach;
    then, at the party, eat somewhat less than you can.
Paris might have hated Helen, had he but seen her
    wolfing down her food. "Stupid thing!" he'd have thought.
Ladies, drinking is better, it's more becoming to women;
    Bacchus and Cupid are two boon companions, it seems.
Yet, make sure your head stays clear, or your feet will go stumbling;
    once your mind's overcome, double vision ensues.
Women who've swilled too much, and just lie there, are ugly to look at;
    women like that deserve going to bed with some lout.
Also, it isn't safe to fall asleep at the table
    after it's cleared; while you sleep, shameful things may occur.

What comes next, I'm ashamed to tell, but fostering Venus
    always says, "If it shames folks, it's my special concern."
Ladies, know yourselves; use personal methods that suit you;
    not all goals can be reached taking a single approach.
Should your face be your fortune, stay on your back when reclining;
    should your back be your best feature, be seen from behind.
Young Milanion bore Atalanta's legs on his shoulders.
    Got good legs? Lift them up lovingly just the same way.
Those who're petite can straddle their man, though Hector's Cilician
    wife, who was much too tall, never used *him* as a horse.
Women whose charm is their long, long sides should kneel on the bedclothes,
    bending their supple neck backward all of the while.
Those with youthful thighs and breasts that are free of a blemish
    ought to lie crosswise; the man ought to stand on his feet.
Also, don't think you'll lose face by letting your hair down the way that
    Laodamia did; bend your neck over your locks.
Should your confinements have left you a belly riddled with wrinkles,

do as the Parthians do: show your backside, instead.
Love has a thousand positions; in one that's not tiring, and simple,
    women lie on their right side, not flat on their back.
Neither Apollo's oracle nor horned Ammon's in Egypt
    utters more truth than does *my* instructional Muse.
Should there be credit in arts that are based on experience, trust them!
    All those poems I wrote ought to attest to my truth.
Let the women, immersed in love to their innermost marrow,
    undergo sex; let one act satisfy female and male.
Don't let persuasive words and mirthgiving murmurs fall silent;
    never refrain from foul language while pumping away.
Women whom fate has denied a natural urge for romancing
    need to pretend that it's fun, uttering amorous sounds.
Luckless that lady must be who's sluggish and numb in the place where
    so much pleasure resides, pleasure for woman and man.
Only, beware, don't be caught in a lie when you do that pretending!
    Let your eyes hint it's real ecstasy—also, your hips!
Let your words and your heavy breathing indicate pleasure;
    also, that bodily part flashes its own secret signs.
After the joys of love, if you ask the man for a present,
    don't expect the request really to carry much weight.
Don't open every window and flood your bedroom with daylight;
    rather, conceal in the shade any bodily faults.

Now our fun's at an end; it's time for releasing the swans that,
    harness strapped to their necks, drew my chariot on.
Just like the men in my first two scrolls, so now let my lady
    pupils write on their spoils: "Ovid taught me all this!"